THE LADY IS A JOCK

To my father and mother

Acknowledgments

I want to thank my editor at Dodd, Mead, who thought up the idea for this book and encouraged me from inception to completion. And particular thanks are also due to Hugh Beeson, Jr. for his conscientious assistance in the book's final stages.

I am deeply grateful to the following: Joe Berger, Mr. & Mrs. Frank Brady, Johnny Campo, Frank Chiaverini, Ken Christopher, Julian Cole, Carole Collins, Lou Cunningham, Randy Cutshaw, Earl Flora, Bill Hartack, Elmer Heubeck, Sam Kanchuger, Jerry Kirschenbaum, William McDonald, Charlie and Lois Meals, Constance Miller, Bill Mulflur, Jim Raftery, Linda Richmond, Dr. Natalie Shainess, Joseph P. Smyth, Dr. Herbert Wieder, Patty Whitmore, and Ed Zneimer.

"Next to horse racing, men are my favorite hobby."
—Jockey Penny Ann Early

"It's like sending a girl out to fight Muhammad Ali."
—A jockey's agent in New Orleans

"I haven't beat up anybody since Toledo."
—Jockey Cheryl White

"The girls add a little tone to the joint."
—A Pinkerton guard at Aqueduct

"I think the convent is probably a hell of a lot rougher."
—Former nun, now jockey Sandy Schleiffers

"It all simmers down to this—would you want your brother to marry a jockey?"
—Sportswriter Red Smith

THE LADY IS A JOCK

1

"If you want something bad enough, I guess you'll do anything. And, Christ, I did! And it was all just to ride!"

—Mary Bacon

At Detroit's Hazel Park Racetrack, it is twenty minutes till post time as the nine jockeys file into the paddock and get ready for the day's seventh race.

Among the cluster of weather-beaten faces and gnomelike bodies strides a stunning girl, a Snow White among the dwarfs. She is in her mid-twenties, and, like her companions, she is slim but strong. Her silky, glimmering blonde hair, accented by reflective gold hoop earrings, provides a striking contrast to the green shamrock pattern of her riding silks. In one hand she carries a Caliente helmet, in the other a whip.

After each jockey takes his place beside the horse he will ride, the paddock judge calls, "Riders up!" and the trainers give their jockeys a "leg-up."

Then, just as the horses start to move onto the track, a voice cries out from the mumbling, dangling conversation. It is one of the "railbirds" who line the fence around the paddock. "Let it all hang out, Lady Godiva!" he yells to the young girl.

"Yeah!" shouts another. "Take off your clothes, Mary! They might put you on the lead!"

Instead of being annoyed, the girl breaks into an impish grin, revealing a straight row of white teeth. Her chocolate-brown eyes sparkle with gaiety as she delights in being in the spotlight.

Not too long before today's race, the jockey, Mary Bacon, posed nude for *Playboy*, and the Detroit newspapers picked it up as a clever news item. The enticing thought of a jockey in the buff brought racing fans out in droves that chilly October day.

After leaving the paddock, Mary's thoughts turn immediately from the crowd to the upcoming race and to her mount, Fortune Cookie. "In the post parade I look for the best part of the track, feel how my horse is warming up, and watch the others I'll have to run against . . . to try to see how much horse they've got under them."

Shortly after the starters at the gate put each horse in its iron cubicle, a bell rings and the track announcer's "They're off!" charges the air with excitement. As the horses tear along the backstretch, Mary fights valiantly to control the half-ton of horseflesh beneath her tiny, one-hundred pound body, her vision half-blinded by the steady tattoo of mud that is kicked up in her face by the front runners.

"I've had to learn to close my mind to pain and cold," Mary admits candidly. "Or else I'd never have made it through the winter meets and broken bones."

Going into the far turn, Mary's horse moves up until it is third.

Noticing that Mary is gaining, the jock in first place looks over his shoulder and yells to the one laying second, "Drop over! Bacon's getting through on the rail!"

Spotting a hole between the two riders, Mary squeezes Fortune Cookie through and flashes across the finish line, barely winning the race in a three-horse finish.

"The kid on the lead was so mad that he took off his mounts for the rest of the day, packed his tack and left Detroit," says Mary, obviously pleased. "I guess he couldn't take it, cause everyone teased him, saying, 'The girl nailed you two on the money.'"

Her energy somewhat drained from the race, Mary slowly pulls Fortune Cookie into the winner's circle, where she is photographed with the horse's owner and trainer. Watching her as she poses at the center of the admiring group—smiling down at one man and then fixing her sexy eyes on another—brings to mind the opening line of *Gone With the Wind*: "Scarlett O'Hara was not beautiful, but men seldom noticed it when caught by her charm."

Like her fictional counterpart, Mary's fascinating charm isn't a bubbly outpouring of warmth; rather, it is a finely polished tool by which she manipulates the men within her sphere and succeeds in getting them to do whatever she bids.

"You're going to name me on another horse tomorrow, aren't you?" Mary asks Fortune Cookie's owner.

"You bet I will!" he replies.

Returning to the makeshift girls' jockey room, Mary begins changing out of her silks.

Close up, the pattern of her flowered bikini panties shows through the white nylon bottoms of her jockey's outfit. "The fans get a kick out of it," Mary laughs as she removes her riding pants. "I'm known for my underpants. I call it 'flower power.' At the gate, the starters will ask me, 'Is it roses or daisies today?' I tell the other jocks, 'At least I give you something to look at when I'm on the lead!'"

Unlike many other girls who are jockeys—there are approximately sixty in the United States today—Mary Bacon strives to be feminine . . . at least on the surface. "I buy all that Revlon crap," she says while scrubbing the last traces of mud from her neck.

"I get up every morning between four and four-fifteen, and I'll tell you that to stand in front of that mirror and draw that little black line and put on all that blue stuff and the rouge and mascara. . . . The whole bit at four in the morning, it's a pain. But I'll tell ya, if you don't take care of yourself, nobody else will.

"And, boy, in a business like this, if I didn't go to bed early every night, put three different types of cream on my face . . . I'd start looking just like an old beaten woman. I guess that's why I ride more than most of the other girls.

"You know, the biggest advantage in riding a girl is that they take better win pictures. Who would want a win picture of a girl when you couldn't tell whether it was or wasn't a girl? Just say that you were a trainer and you named a girl jockey on your horse. And the owners came to the races that day and they happened to notice that a girl was going to ride their horse. Well, when they walked into that paddock, they'd sure rather see some pretty little girl get on that horse than some ugly dyke."

She slid into a pair of slick, clean Levis and pulled on a hot pink turtleneck sweater. The final accents were a Stetson hat and a pair of boots that would do Roy Rogers proud. "I'm just a little ol' cowgirl," she said, smiling as she strutted out of the dressing room.

Maybe so. But it's a rare "little ol' cowgirl" who has experienced a life as fast and as wild as Mary Bacon has in her short years. If she doesn't kill herself before she reaches thirty, she might win a lasting niche in American folklore.

Mary has broken her collarbone, her back, several ribs, both hands and both feet. She has punctured a lung and suffered numerous concussions. "I got a lot of bones that aren't connected. That just flip around." She's also ridden when she was seven months pregnant, and she rode after a maniac stable groom tried to kill her. "It's all for the love of a horse," she says—with just the smallest touch of bitterness.

Of all the female jockeys who succeeded in getting a license when racing lowered its sex barrier in 1969, Mary is one of the few who have displayed both the talent and the toughness to ride regularly against men and to make a mark. Of the girls now racing on pari-mutuel tracks throughout the country, only a small number ride on what might be termed a "daily basis." George Stidham, the Eastern representative of the Jockeys Association, says of Mary Bacon, "It's not fair to judge her with girl riders. She's about half-guy. She's the toughest broad I ever seen on a horse."

Mary agrees. "I ride very hard and very strong. I can

actually crucify a horse. I should get an Academy Award. I'm probably the greatest actress that ever came along because I can paint myself up and look like a girl, but underneath I take that makeup off and pull back my hair and put that helmet on and I'm really a man. I think I'm a female impersonator." The role she plays is not an easy one. "It's hard to be a man and a woman at the same time," Mary has said. "And I've been a man for so long. On a horse I become so masculine."

While Mary is still not in the Bill Shoemaker-Braulio Baeza class, she is doing well, literally holding her own at the medium-size tracks in the Middle West and in the South where she usually races.

Mary's most lucrative victory was a $30,000 quarter horse race in Oklahoma of which she received ten percent. But last spring she also had mounts in two prestigious races, the Spendthrift and the Phoenix, at Keeneland in Kentucky. And she almost rode in the 1972 Kentucky Derby. Her horse, Bold Music, was entered, only to be scratched early during Derby Week. Nevertheless, Mary Bacon still gets more 20-to-1 shots than she does favorites, thereby making her life a ceaseless hustle.

Mary started riding in horse shows when she was five years old. By the time she was nine, she was racing quarter horses and Appaloosas at the backwood bush tracks of Oklahoma, where women, much less little girls, were a rarity.

Anything goes in the "bushes," the small racetracks, often situated on fairgrounds, which are not subject to the jurisdictions of state racing commissions. Often the races are run surreptitiously in such states as Georgia and Texas, where legal betting is not permitted. Kicking, punching and dropping in front of another jockey are common occurrences. "The guys would think nothing of carrying chains, or even joints, to make those cripples go," says Mary. A "joint" or "buzzer" is an electrical device that shocks a horse into running faster. It is outlawed on pari-mutuel tracks.

In the rough-and-tumble, carnival atmosphere of the bush tracks, the bettors will put their money on anything, if only for a laugh. "I rode in a quarter horse race one time," Mary recalls, "and on one side of me they had a chicken tied to the saddle. On the other side they had tin cans tied on. I guess the guy who put me on his horse figured I was as good as a chicken."

Throughout her childhood and adolescence, Mary rode horses in the bushes, in horse shows and in rodeos, where she also once rode a Brahman bull. Horses were the one consistently good thing that happened to Mary while she was growing up. The rest of her life, according to her, was "miserable." Even now, when she talks about it, her voice sinks into a sad monotone. "I don't like to talk about my childhood," she says.

Mary's father was part of a carnival family. Her mother's parents owned a small horse and cattle farm. "I'm like a horse that's not well-bred" is Mary's way of describing her origins. "I'm by a carny out of a hillbilly," she says, adding, "Sometimes not a top stud produces a real runner."

About her mother, Mary's opinion is candid and, in its

way, amusing: "She was beautiful until she opened her mouth. She was not formally educated. She was illiterate, but she was a very nice person." Though spoken in the past tense, Mary's mother is still very much alive.

When Mary was a child, her father sometimes worked as a pianist while her mother sometimes modeled and sang in nightclubs in Chicago. As a little girl, Mary had swimming and ballet lessons. And she owned a horse.

Then her father "became undone," as Mary phrases it, and was unemployed for long periods of time; when he did have a job, he wouldn't, or couldn't, hold it. Sometimes he'd join a rodeo and stay with it a few months; at other times he'd become involved in "business deals" that were never discussed with Mary or with her sister or brother. "If the truth were known," she says, "he would probably be in jail." In her own way, Mary understands her father's weaknesses. "When he broke down, he just couldn't face reality and he turned to liquor. It was the wall he was hiding behind, just like horses are the wall I'm hiding behind."

Throughout the many lean times, Mary's mother tried desperately to keep the family together. "I remember one time my mother worked in a bean camp with migratory farmers. She would come home and her hands would be all ragged from shelling the beans. Before that she used to have long red fingernails."

Life was in a state of constant confusion, with the children ricocheting from school to school as the family moved from place to place. Mary lived in Illinois, Oklahoma, New Mexico, Minnesota and Michigan while growing up. When she was twelve she was farmed out for a year to a Mrs. Maryann Wanatick in New Mexico.

Mary hated that. "I remember one time being really sick and wanting my mother so bad. And I didn't even know where she was."

Mary's opinion of foster homes is not the usual one. "In a foster home they've got you there for some reason. *Not* usually because they are so good-hearted, but because they got a free baby-sitter and all they got to do is slip some cheap meat and some canned vegetables in front of you at night. Or someone to clean the house or something like that."

Mrs. Wanatick really loved Mary, she says, and it's obvious that Mary was fond of her too; but with distance. "Mrs. Wanatick liked playing with makeup and all that, and she really taught me a lot," Mary recalls.

Even as a young girl, Mary Bacon was a hell-raiser. One night, while living with Mrs. Wanatick, she was shot in the leg as she stole a neighbor's watermelon. "We used to steal them and take them out on the highway and break them open. At night they'd be cold inside and, boy, were they good!"

After Mary was reunited with her real family, she often ran away. "My sister and I were notorious for running away from home," she admits. But for Mary, running away meant running to a stable.

Whenever she is upset, Mary retreats into her world of horses. For her it is a private world, a very real one. "It was like sleeping overnight with one of my girl friends. I had this one horse that I used to tell all my problems to. At night, I'd lie down in the stall and sleep on his neck."

Mary would always be found, of course, and frequently she was sent to a reform school. The first time this happened was while she was living in New Mexico.

"It was the first time in my life that I had a dress on," she says. "The dress was the kind with two big holes in front for your arms and it wrapped around and tied in the back. I used to lie on my cot in that stupid cell and count the blocks. There were 247 blocks up and 283 blocks wide. I used to watch the cockroaches go up the walls. You get schooled awful fast. I learned to lie and to steal and to cheat and to fight. And I'll tell you something. There's a lot of times someone thinks they can whip me . . . well, they'll come out with the scars!"

Once Mary was confined three months for stealing some chickens. "Me and this kid were stealing chickens. We stole twenty-three and stuck them in these gunnysacks. That was in Oklahoma. They were squawking and making all kinds of noise, and we were dragging them down the highway because we were going to try to sell them. We saw an old pick-up truck by the side of the road, and the kid with me said, 'Hey, I bet I can get that thing going!' I don't know if there was a key in it or a hot wire, but he got that truck moving. In the back was a big box where they put tools and things, and we put the chickens in there.

"So we can't hear the back of the truck while we're driving because it's so noisy and bumpy. Then the kid runs a goddamned stop sign next to this drive-in restaurant where there was a cop sitting, and he chased us. Naturally, the cop asked for a driver's license. We were both fourteen years old, and didn't have no driver's license. Then the cop asked him for the papers on the truck. Well the truck, of course, was stolen. Next he looked in the back of the truck and the twenty-three chickens was smothered. So that was that."

At fifteen, Mary was living with her family again, this time in Elk City, Oklahoma. And in the same year she received her first recognition, her first singular honor. She was elected Snow Queen in a local contest—a fact that still surprises her a bit, for she remembers her high school years as being basically lonely and friendless. Mary socialized very little while in school. "Half the kids weren't allowed to associate with me," she says, "because I hung out at the racetracks."

The irony of this came back a few years later, just after Mary had begun to achieve some fame and recognition as a jockey. "One time one of the girls from the high school came up to me after a race in Toledo. She was with some friends and she yelled, 'Mary! Mary! Remember me?' 'I don't know you, lady,' I said. I remembered the way she once turned up her nose at me."

Mary finished school in 1966, when she was fifteen years old. "I cheated all the way through. I don't know why they ever passed me." Mary has often regretted not taking advantage of her educational opportunity, and after she became a jockey, she put her younger brother through a Catholic prep school, paying $375 a semester.

When she was sixteen, Mary saw and fell in love with *The Horsemaster*, a Walt Disney movie. The story takes place at the Porelock Vale Riding School in Somerset, England. After seeing the film, Mary became obsessed with the desire to learn steeplechase riding. Without any money, she applied to the school and was accepted for the January term.

At an early age, her catalog of jobs was both colorful and memorable. "When I left home I worked as a lifeguard during the day, and at night I rode in harness meets at Raceway Park." The fall before she was to go to England, Mary galloped horses from five to eight-thirty in the morning, then did odd jobs at the Grosse Pointe Hunt Club in Detroit from nine until six in the evening. Three nights a week she worked as a go-go dancer at the Continental Hotel. "By two in the morning, they'd close the doors. They had gambling and all that stuff in there."

Despite her several jobs, Mary was still not earning enough to pay the tuition at Porelock Vale. So on nights when she wasn't dancing at the Continental Hotel, she hired herself out to private parties, where for anywhere from twenty-five to seventy-five dollars, depending on the generosity of the host, she jumped topless out of cakes. "If you want something bad enough, I guess you'll do anything," Mary reasoned. "And, Christ, I did! And it was all just to ride!"

Pastry-popping is a somewhat specialized field, and people remember you. Several years later, after Mary had become an established jockey, she was sitting with her agent in the posh Detroit Racecourse Club. A number of prominent businessmen were present. One, a glint of recognition appearing in his eyes, smiled and said, "*Now* I know where I've seen you! You were the girl in the cake!"

"You must be mistaken," Mary replied, somewhat flustered.

"No, you're the one," he insisted. "You used to wiggle yourself so cute."

Mary did make it to Porelock Vale, where she studied stable management, veterinary medicine and steeplechase riding. At the end of the academic year, she took the horsemanship examination administered by the British government. She passed, receiving a certificate designating her as a British Horse Society Assistant.

Upon her return to the United States, in the summer of 1967, Mary was rehired by the Grosse Pointe Hunt Club, where she taught riding to wealthy socialites. Among her students was Mrs. Christina Ford. And she also worked galloping horses for Pete Maxwell, one of the country's top trainers.

Working for Pete at the same time was a "bug boy" named Johnny Bacon. On the program at thoroughbred racetracks, the weight citation carried by the horse is sometimes preceded by a printed asterisk (*) or two asterisks (**) or even three (***). These symbols indicate that the horse is being ridden by an apprentice jockey and therefore has received a special weight allowance. An asterisk looks like a bug walking across the program—hence, the weight allowance has come to be known as a "bug," and the apprentice as a "bug boy" or "bug rider."

An apprentice is literally an inexperienced kid, usually one too green to compete on an equal basis with experienced, professional riders in race after race. Because he is so inexperienced, the racing rules allow his employers extra weight off their horses as an inducement to hire him. An apprentice is permitted to carry ten pounds less weight than his horse would carry if it were being ridden by a fully qualified rider.

An apprentice is permitted a 10-pound weight allowance until he has five wins; 7 pounds for his next thirty-five wins; and 5 pounds after that or until a year from his first win. If the apprentice then continues to ride for the contract holder for whom he rode his first win, he is permitted a 3 pound allowance for one additional year.

Johnny Bacon was not an unfamiliar face to Mary. She had first known him in Oklahoma, where they met as teenagers when both were breaking from the gate at a bush race just outside Elk City.

Three weeks and two days after they reestablished their friendship in Detroit, Mary and Johnny eloped to Canadian, Texas. They were married by a justice of the peace. "We galloped twenty-seven horses that morning," Mary recalls. "I had on a pair of tan Levis. Somebody gave them to me, and they were too big. I also had on a cowboy hat. We drove over state lines and we got some grooms to act as our parents because we didn't want our real parents to know. One groom was so drunk that he spelled Johnny's father's name wrong on the marriage license. They gave us the blood test the same day, and the whole thing only cost twenty-two dollars."

Johnny Bacon is a skinny kid with a cute pug face. He walks with the conceited strut of a rock 'n' roll star and, like Mary, seems to have within himself a wild streak just itching to burst forth. His parents were migrant farmers, and both his mother and his father have been married three times.

Mary worshipped Johnny Bacon, and she still does. Like horses, he became another of her fanatical obsessions. According to Mary, she was the giver in their marriage, while Johnny was always ready to take. "He never bought me a wedding ring. He's got a ring that he still wears that's got twenty-one diamonds in it. I bought it for him with money I made riding. Johnny never gave me a Christmas present or a birthday present."

Johnny was the leading apprentice rider in the country when they married, and, as his wife, Mary proudly and happily followed him from track to track. "We were closer than man and wife," Mary recalled later. "We were more like brother and sister. Johnny was me and I was him. I wore his clothes and he wore mine. And when we got mad at each other, we'd have regular fist fights."

Wherever Johnny raced, Mary got jobs exercising horses during the morning or working as a pony girl in the afternoon. (Exercisers gallop horses; pony girls or boys lead horses to the gate before a race.)

Like many other unestablished jockeys, Johnny Bacon also galloped horses. The work provided extra cash, but it was a job he didn't like.

"I was such a sucker," Mary said when thinking of her days as a newlywed. "Johnny would lie in bed and say, 'Awwww, I don't feel well today. Go out and get on my horses.'"

And Mary would, of course. She got up early every morning and galloped her horses as well as Johnny's. Then she ponied them in the afternoon and later cooked dinner and did the laundry. "His Levis had to be starched just so. I did everything, like a dumb ass!"

Mary remembers her marriage well. "When I married Johnny Bacon, he had two pairs of Levis and a couple of red Western shirts. After we'd been married for a while, all *his* clothes were custom-made. His exercise boots cost $125. They were brown alligator with wing tips. Everything was monogrammed. He had his suits made in Montreal. They were $350 to $400, and he wore diamond rings and diamond watches and drove a big car. You know, I had to laugh."

There were times, though, when Mary couldn't laugh. Johnny hadn't married Julia Child, nor was Mary "Craig's wife." "Off the track I'm lost," says Mary. It's a common confession among the girl jockeys. "Oh, I know how to mix feed, but I don't really know how to cook. And I can muck out a stall, but I don't know how to clean house."

Early in 1969, after the Bacons had been married for a little more than a year, Mary learned she was pregnant. Her father's reaction to the news was somewhat unusual, and Mary quotes him with amusement: "I know Mary never went to bed with Johnny. She conceived this baby alone." And he honestly believed that, Mary recalls, because he'd say, "I know my little girl Mary would never do that."

Mary has mixed feelings about her father. His death was a hard blow to her. "I can't face reality. And I never could. I never went to the mortuary or anything like that. Because if I ever saw him dead, then I would realize that he *was* dead.

So in the back of my mind he's still alive." Her father died nearly four years ago, and she raced the day he was buried. The memory of that race is vivid. "When you are coming down the lane, you can hear the roar of the crowd, the cheering. You don't hear separate voices, individual ones. But I heard a voice yell, 'Come on, Mary!' And I looked over my shoulder and I swear to God I saw my father standing there with a little girl."

Just as Mary's feelings about her father are unsettled, so too are her feelings about Johnny. "It used to kill me to take Johnny to the post. One day I was sitting out on the pony. Knocked up. Carrying Suzie. And it's muddy and my pony's full of mud and I'm full of mud. I was sitting in the paddock, waiting to take Johnny to the post to run a race. And there was a couple of girls in their little short skirts and their hair ratted up a mile, and when he came riding out one of them said, 'Isn't he cute!' And the other said, 'Oh, hi! Johnny!' And I wanted to say, 'You dumb bitches! That Oklahoma hill-billy's my husband! You think he's so cute and so smart. Well, he was in the sixth grade when he was sixteen years old!'

"Sixteen years old and still in the sixth grade," Mary repeated.

The girl jockey craze hit the nation while Mary was pregnant. The brouhaha was started by Kathy Kusner, an Olympic rider who sued for, and won, the right to ride in the state of Maryland, only to injure her leg in a horse show at Madison Square Garden and thus invalidate her chances before she even broke from a starting gate.

Next came a pretty blonde, Penny Ann Early, quickly dubbed the "country's shapliest jockey" by *The New York Times*. Four times Penny Ann tried to race against the boys at Churchill Downs, and each time she was met by boycotts and nasty accusations labeling her a publicity seeker. Temporarily defeated, Penny Ann abandoned racing and limped off to play basketball for the financially sagging Kentucky Colonels. Regarding her qualifications for that, she was succinct. "I played in high school," she told a reporter. "It was in gym class."

Everybody had an opinion on the subject of girl jockeys. Nick James, president of the Jockeys Guild, called them "jockettes" and termed the invasion a "mockery of Thoroughbred Horseracing," predicting ominously of "female blood being spilled on American racetracks."

Sportswriter Red Smith saw things from a somewhat different angle. "It all simmers down to this—would you want your brother to marry a jockey?"

Slowly, some of the male jockeys relented, or at least seemed to. They assumed, albeit erroneously, that once the girls got out on the track and were knocked around a bit, they'd hang up their tack.

The major breakthrough came on February 7, 1969, when Diane Crump donned her silks and, without any opposition from the male contingent, rode against the boys at Hialeah.

Later that month, shy, nineteen-year-old Barbara Jo Rubin mounted a colt named Cohesion at Charles Town, West Virginia, and, before a record-breaking crowd, rode to a smashing victory, thus marking herself as the first woman in American history to win against men in a professional sport.

Barbara Jo became a phenomenon, an overnight celebrity. Charles Town presented her with a real Camaro, as a thank you gesture for all the publicity she had brought to them. Pimlico gave her a mink stole. She later raced—and won—at Aqueduct, where she was flanked by guards to keep the crowd from tearing at her clothes, which, in a typically American acknowledgement of celebrity, they wanted for souvenirs. She appeared on *The Ed Sullivan Show, The Kraft Music Hall* and *The Today Show.*

Reading about these girls in the newspapers, seeing them on television and hearing all the banter around the tracks increased Mary's anxieties. She had more than simply an urge or a burning desire to compete. She had the talent and the ability. In fact, she knew she could win.

Even though she continued to gallop horses while she was pregnant, and even though she would race while pregnant again after she became a jockey, Mary Bacon, with all her moxie and determination, could not bring herself to walk into the steward's office and apply for a jockey's license with her femininity bulgingly apparent.

Mary and Johnny's daughter, Susan Michaela, was born on March 4, 1969. Seven days later, Mary was back galloping horses.

The first mount she had when she did receive her license was for Pete Maxwell. "He threw me up on the horse," Mary remembers. "I was used to galloping horses, but in racing your rear end isn't sitting on the saddle. As a jockey you're crouched down, but your rear isn't sitting. You're sort of perched on top of the saddle. So I figured I could do it because my rear wouldn't be touching. But the first horse I got on . . . Well, Pete threw me up and I landed on the horse's back and the horse flipped over and landed right on top of me. He was 'cold back.' That means a soft back. It's goosey-like. He was spooky." In racing slang, a horse that is called spooky overreacts to stimuli. If he spots a piece of paper on the track, for example, he will bolt and veer off the course.

The shock is memorable even today. "I'd had 283 internal stitches and a whole rear end full of external ones when I had Suzie. I went back to the hospital because I'd torn my external stitches, and, boy, they didn't even use any anesthesia!

"Two years later that horse that flipped over backwards on me was one of my mounts, and I won a race on him. It's a small world. I run into horses all the time that I rode four or five years ago. And people say it's funny, how you see your friends end up in life. Well, to me it's funny how I see my horses end up. I knew some of them a couple of years ago when they were allowance, and now they're running for a tag. It's just like people saying that they knew friends when they were big bosses and now they're on skid row . . . Well, I've seen horses that were in stakes races and now they're on skid row."

In May, 1969, Mary received her license at Finger Lakes, New York.

The memory of her first race is still vivid. "When that overnight came out (the overnight is a schedule of races posted forty-eight hours in advance), and it said, 'JOCKEY: MARY BACON,' for two days I was having a heart attack. But as soon as they threw me up on that horse, everything went out of my mind except for winning that race."

Like all jockeys applying for their jockey's license, Mary's first two races were monitored by the stewards to determine whether they should give her one. She placed second in her first race. The next time out, she "broke her maiden," which in backstretch argot means she won the race.

Pete Maxwell signed her to a three-year contract, while giving her the option to freelance for other trainers as much as she chose.

Because it is completely binding throughout the world of thoroughbred racing, a jockey's contract may be the closest link to legal serfdom in America. In most states the rules of racing do not refer to the apprentice as being "hired" or "employed." Instead, they note that he has "bound himself" to his boss—which means the boss can control the mounts the jockey gets. This also means that he can require the apprentice to work seven days a week, at low wages, and that he can closely regulate the jockey's personal life. A trainer, for example, can forbid a jockey to go out at night or even to own an automobile.

The apprentice jockey is unlike most other athletes in that he has not learned, or polished, his trade in high school or college. He actually learns it on the job, and the investment in his education must be recovered by his teacher. Most jockeys in America today are relatively young, and most are high school dropouts. Many are ill-suited to handle large sums of money; it is not an uncommon incident for some to wager their whole paycheck.

To become a jockey one has to be at least sixteen years old and, if under legal age, has to have parental consent. He is then placed under the care of a licensed owner or trainer who supervises his (or her) training. He must be willing, literally, to start at the bottom, which means cleaning stalls, soaping leather halters and saddles and bridles, and cooling hot horses after they have worked out or have raced. There is little glamour in the job of a beginner. For a woman it is sometimes more demanding, as Donna Hillman has commented: "With a girl they can say, 'Lie down or you will have to muck out stalls.' "

In addition to all the physical requirements, a jockey must be intelligent, perceptive and, of course, daring. If he isn't brave, he isn't going to make it.

True to all predictions, Mary Bacon turned out to be a feisty, high-spirited little jockey. "I'll do anything to win," is her credo.

Her determination was recognized wherever she raced. "I rode a race one time with a kid, and as we were coming down the line, we were head to head. All the way down the track I was beating him on the head and beating his horse on the head. I won the race, but after we went over the finish line, he crashed his horse into mine and we both went off."

Often Johnny would be standing around the recreation room in the male jockeys' quarters, and would overhear some of the comments made by his comrades after they returned from racing against his wife. "I remember one time I was playin' pool with another jock, and he called Mary a hard-assed broad. I knocked him down with a cue stick."

Such chivalry was perhaps unwarranted. In the few times that Mary rode against her husband, she was just as rough on him as she was on the other riders.

Once, during a race at Hazel Park, Mary became angry at Johnny during the post parade and ran him into a rail. "He ended up winning the race and I finished fourth. They gave me five days for rough riding, but when we got home he got five nights. He made it look worse than it was, complaining and screaming to the stewards."

The Bacons seldom raced against each other because most tracks frown upon such an idea. If an accident happened, it would be difficult for one to testify against the other. So Mary and Johnny usually raced at different tracks and commuted to be together on their days off.

The more Mary rode, the greater her desire became to improve her technique. Her years of galloping quarter horses in the bush meets had provided invaluable experience, but racing with thoroughbreds on pari-mutuel tracks proved to be a new challenge. Good jockeys must have superior reflexes and excellent nerve control. They must know how to work fast under intense pressure and be able to make split-second decisions—correct ones. Timing, obviously, is also important. Knowing how fast the horses in front are running is just as vital as knowing how one's own horse is running; each rider must be able to rate his own mount as he gallops around the course.

A really good jockey has a built-in clock in his head that tells him how fast his horse is going. Knowing this, he tries not to exhaust the animal before the final stretch. The rider must also be able to count off second by second just how long it is taking his mount to run between the poles that mark each sixteenth of a mile on the track. Most importantly, a jockey must have balance at all times. He has to be able to bob and to weave his body as he rides neck and neck down the stretch.

And, of course, jockeys are not unlike other people in that they all have different personalities; some are thin-skinned just as others are thick. Some are narrow and quite prejudiced, while others are liberal and understanding. Their private, intense lives are a microcosm of the world at large.

Mary has said that she wouldn't dream of trading her skinny, flat-chested body for Raquel Welch's ample abundance, because a big bust makes it difficult to hug a horse's neck and a curvy behind might upset her balance.

In a short time, Mary's total devotion to riding began to pay off. Even though she only began riding in May, 1969, by the end of that year she had ridden three times as many races and won three times as many as any of the other girl riders. After only six months she was the thirteenth leading "bug boy" in the United States.

A trainer who encountered Mary frequently on the racing circuit soapboxes enthusiastically: "Mary's not afraid to go anywhere and try to ride. A lot of jockeys will only go where their contract holder or their agent sends them. Not Mary! She'll walk on a track cold turkey and say, 'Boys, here I am!

I want to ride!' She'll start galloping horses in the morning, and the first thing you know, you'll start seeing her name in the program in the afternoon."

Whenever possible, Mary tried to work as many tracks as she could. She rode during the day in Cleveland and at night at Waterford Park in West Virginia; days in Lexington, Kentucky, and nights in neighboring Latonia. When she was riding at Tropical Park, she was racing for a man who owned a plane, and he would fly her to Orlando, where she'd race at night.

Like the other girls on the racing circuit, Mary must frequently change in the ladies room or in the first-aid room, for most tracks still do not have quarters for women. In Florida, many retired persons spend the day at the track; and one afternoon, when Mary was racing at Tropical Park, an elderly spectator had a fatal heart attack and was placed in the first-aid room, which was where Mary was supposed to dress. "I'm not changing in front of a dead man," Mary said to the management.

In spite of all her bravura, her spunk and her ability to roll with the punches and the kicks, Mary has usually been a woman alone and, thus, an easy mark for racing's bad elements. Tracks are known—especially among the people who work at them—to be frequented by some pretty disreputable characters, who are attracted because they find comfort in the seedy, free atmosphere. Here they feel at home.

The gypsy life of the racing world is both a natural magnet and a natural habitat for drifters, many of whom are consistently on the skids. Jobs under the shed rows on the backside pay so little and involve such inconvenient hours that, until recently when women began to fill these positions, trainers were often faced with no other choice than hiring winos, alcoholics, drifters and pill poppers to look after the horses. Because thoroughbreds require constant care, a groom is usually needed in the stable and most often sleeps there. There aren't many persons who will take such a job nowadays for $75 to $125 a week.

Paul Corley Turner was a drifter who worked in the shed row next to where Mary used to gallop horses at Pocono Downs in Pennsylvania. And for some unhappy reason, he fastened on Mary Bacon. "He was the kind of person you look at and fear," she says. "He had a purplish cast to his skin, like he had a heart condition or something. And he had hardly any hair, which made him look like he was all face."

One morning while she was riding to the track with Roy Court, her agent, Paul saw them. He flagged them down and asked for a ride. Shortly after he got into the car, he pulled a knife and forced them into a nearby woods. Then he locked Roy in the trunk and grabbed Mary. He threw her to the ground, put the knife at her throat and told her that he was going to disfigure her. Mary struggled free. A chase ensued down railroad tracks and up a hill. Turner caught her; she kicked him in the shoulder and he threw the knife. Mary fled again, made her way through a fallen barbed wire fence and eventually found the highway, where she hitched a ride to the track.

In the meantime, Court had freed himself, using a penknife to pry open the latch of the trunk. He sped back to the track and called the police. Mary showed up not too long after, dazed and somewhat frightened by her ordeal.

She was harassed that afternoon by reporters from the newspapers and the local television stations, all wanting to know first-hand the gruesome details. Mary's mother learned of the experience not from Mary, who hadn't had time to call, but from the six o'clock news when her daughter flashed on the TV screen.

True to form, Mary's exhaustion—such as it was—proved only temporary. She raced that night.

Both the Associated Press and United Press International, the country's two major wire services, reported the story, as did *The New York Times*. Not to be outdone, a national weekly tabloid that specializes in the sensational, rewrote the story to serve its own sleazy purposes. As their staff writer saw it, Mary Bacon was a sex-starved jockey who led Paul into the woods, where he struggled against the advances of this flat-chested girl. The story was headlined: "Was the Bacon Too Lean for Paul?"

Turner was tracked down by the police two months later in Tampa, Florida, and was extradicted to Pennsylvania. Mary had been riding at so many different tracks that the authorities couldn't find her. At the time of the trial, she was racing in Caracas, Venezuela, with Diane Crump and Robyn Smith, so she did not testify. Turner was sentenced to only four months.

Mary accepted this unfortunate incident as simply over when it ended. She assumed after Turner's arrest and sentence that he wouldn't dare approach her again. But she was wrong.

After the Turner trouble, it occurred to Mary that two women traveling together might be safer than one. Besides, she was lonely, often coming home to an empty motel room. The nightly routine of television and sparse meals held little appeal for her.

While she was racing in Latonia, Kentucky, Mary met a groom, Judy Wilson, with whom she became friends. She asked Judy to be her agent, and Judy accepted. "Judy and I lived together for two years. She was like the wife and I was like the husband. I made the living and I went out and rode the races. She did the laundry and kept the house." Judy also baby-sat with Suzie.

When a woman becomes involved in a masculine profession, people are frequently quick to assume that she must be a lesbian. The thought also occurs to many lesbians.

"A lot of folks think I'm queer," Mary says. "I used to have a couple of queers in New York who would stand along the fence. And they used to flirt with me. I just went along with them and laughed."

A person like Mary Bacon has been forced by circumstances to become so strong in her everyday nature that the same nature often strives for something stronger than even most men can provide. So she is literally compelled to reject the traditional woman's role and forced to exercise all the prerogatives that are usually considered male domain—warrior, bread winner, decisionmaker.

These are the new women, the new pioneers. And cast in

such a role, Mary could no longer play at being a traditional wife to Johnny. She had grown up seeing her father as a weak man, and therefore nearly all men seemed weak. Mary was often forced to bail Johnny out financially. The simple job of getting up and exercising *his* horses in the morning was a blow to her independence.

When a woman is successful in a man's world—either thrust into it by choice or else by circumstances beyond her control—she often emerges stronger than a man. Mary Bacon doesn't want to "put men down." Instead she is looking for a personality stronger than herself. She uses all her feminine assets as ploys; just as posing for *Playboy* was nothing more than a means to further her own ends. If she uses others, however, she also uses herself in the process.

In 1970 Mary became pregnant for the second time. The news did not make her especially happy. "When something happens that I don't like, I just pretend it's not happening," she says. "And that's how it was with the baby."

Mary was still living with Johnny when the second pregnancy occurred. She was a "stupid kid," she said and never took the Pill after Suzie's birth because she didn't think another pregnancy could come for quite a while. Actually, she figures she became pregnant about eight weeks after Suzie was born.

Mary gained only five pounds. But she is small, and as the months progressed, her condition began to show. She was riding at Raceway Park in Toledo. Since it was winter, all the jockeys wore coats or jackets under their silks. "Some of the jocks were eyeing me kind of funny, but nobody really knew and I got away with it." Mary rode until the seventh month. Once she even rode a horse in foal. The four of them finished last.

"I remember the day she had the baby," Judy Wilson says. "She was named on five mounts, and while she was riding on the third one, she started to lose water and she went into labor right there on the horse."

Mary was rushed to a hospital, where she gave birth to a son. The twenty-four-ounce child died within a few minutes. "It took them two and a half hours to get it out of me because it got hung up in my pelvic bones and came out breech," Mary recalled, wincing as she remembered the pain.

While Mary was recuperating, Judy went to Seminole in Orlando, Florida, and whipped up the track's publicity department. The thought of having the country's leading girl jockey at their track, plus the fact that she had just lost a baby while racing, was surely good for some space in the newspapers. Judy also hustled mounts for her client.

"The day I got out of the hospital," Mary recalls, "I packed the car and drove all the way down to Orlando. Drove straight through. Got there at four-thirty in the morning. An hour later I was on my first horse. Worked eleven horses that morning, did publicity in the afternoon and then went to the dog races."

By post time, the strain had sapped her energy and Mary wasn't up to riding. But she rode anyway. The first horse bolted all the way from the rail to the fence. The second one fell on her.

When Mary regained her energy, she poured even more of

her physical and emotional resources into racing. Horses had always been a substitute for her inability to deal with people, and now she rode them with a vengeance. "If you take a person and do everything in the world for them, chances are they'll stab you in the back," she rationalizes. "You take a horse and feed him and he'll run his heart out for you."

The only persons she has ever been really close to are Johnny and Judy and Jack Van Berg, a trainer. Understandably, Johnny considered her antics such as riding while pregnant a rejection of her duties as wife and mother. Although Mary held on to Johnny for emotional support—sometimes—she remembered the pain of two distressful labors and came to associate the act of sex with this pain. So when Johnny came to see her, she tried to avoid going to bed with him; and if called on, turned her thoughts to thoroughbreds. "Johnny'd be making love to me and I'd be thinking about the horses I was going to ride the next day."

Mary Bacon's thoughts about sex are as unusual as she is: "For me, I don't dig sex. I don't get that much out of it. I guess it's in my subconscious or something, but always in the back of my mind is the pain I went through having a baby."

After racing at Orlando, Mary and Judy moved on to Beulah Park in Ohio, where Mary again encountered Paul Turner. He was not over his obsession. When Mary went into the track kitchen for breakfast and Paul was there, he would always sit near her.

And sometimes, usually in the middle of the night, her telephone would ring. Turner would say to her, "Ma . . . rrrry, I'm going to kill you. I don't want to kill you, but I'm going to *have* to kill you." Instead of reporting these calls, Mary tried to forget about them, to blot them from her mind.

On May 25, 1971, Mary and Judy moved to Churchill Downs, where they rented a room at the Colony Motel on the Dixie Highway. When they returned to the motel after the opening night of the races, they saw a light shining in their bathroom. The rest of the room was dark.

Mary grabbed a pair of scissors that were on top of the dresser and kicked the bathroom door open. Paul Turner leaped out, armed with a gun.

Just as he fired, Mary ducked. The bullet flew past Judy's head, grazing the side of her face. Turner fired again, and this time the bullet singed Judy's neck before it lodged in her hand.

Mary grabbed Judy and headed for the door, but Judy fell over a suitcase. As she lay on the floor, Turner put the gun to her temple and again pulled the trigger.

Mercifully, the gun jammed.

He ran out the door.

Mary and Judy reported the incident to the police, who, after an extensive search, could not locate Paul Turner.

But Mary always felt his presence. "If you want to think of something that will blow your mind," she says, "you ought to walk out of your hotel room one day and find a bullet sitting on the hood of your car. Just to remind you there's a killer out there somewhere, looking for you."

Then the girls took the case to the FBI, who said the only way they could capture him was during an interstate flight.

In the ensuing months, Turner called Mary and Judy and repeatedly threatened them. They had no idea where he was until he wrote to Mary one day in August asking her to write to him. She was to send the letter to "Earl Crook," in care of general delivery, Chicago.

Mary telephoned the FBI, who brought over some brightly colored stationery for Mary to use when answering Paul Turner's request. Then the FBI posted two men at the main Chicago post office. They waited for Paul to pick up the letter, counting on the bright paper to help them spot him. Turner picked up the letter and was followed to his apartment by the FBI, who arrested him. That was in September, 1971.

On January 27, 1972, Turner went on trial, charged with burglary and malicious shooting and wounding. He was sentenced on both charges and is now serving twelve years at the federal penitentiary in Frankfort, Kentucky.

There is, perhaps, a violent side to Mary's character which attracted Paul Turner. "I was a toner to Mary's personality," Judy says. "She has a very violent personality." Mary's description of her own personality is precise. "I'm a good friend but a bad enemy," she says. "I guess that's why I can ride a racehorse, because I can be very vicious."

Like a hero in a Western movie, Mary Bacon's first instincts tell her to slug first and talk later.

Not too long after the harrowing night with Paul Turner, Mary was pulling out of the parking lot at Churchill Downs when a traffic policeman gestured for her to go left instead of right. "I thought he was just a rent-a-cop. You know, one of those guards they hire to work at the track," Mary said when explaining why she continued to go right.

The cop got on his motorcycle and overtook Mary, who

was rushing away. When he recognized her as the jockey who rode a horse that he had bet on that day, he flipped Mary's cowboy hat down on her face and said, "Hey, Annie Oakley, you either rode a bad horse in that race or you're awfully strong." To Mary that was an intimation that she had deliberately held off, that she had restrained her mount in order to collect a payoff.

"I hauled off and hit him in the mouth and he started to bleed. Then I kicked him in the shins."

At first under arrest for going through a police barricade, Mary was now charged with assaulting an officer.

At the Louisville jail that night, Judy tried unsuccessfully to have two bondsmen bail her out.

"Each time Mary went before the chief of police, she'd cuss him out and he'd slap another fine on her," recalls Judy. "Finally, by 4 A.M., the bondsmen got disgusted and went home. I ended up having to fork out $500 of my own money for her."

"She had the $500 that night," Mary says, "because I'd got paid and she'd picked up the check. The bond was $5000, of which Judy paid 10 percent."

As a result of these incidents, a court trial took place. Mary smiles recalling the event. "When the judge asked that cop what happened, he said, 'She hit me.' The courtroom busted up. He must have weighed 260 and I was 97 pounds at the time." The judge fined Mary eleven dollars and returned the five hundred.

Sometimes Mary directed her fighting nature toward the other girl jockeys. She got along with very few of them, and few got along with her. This she admits freely. "Most of the girls I can't stand. I don't trust them. Women are vicious people."

Part of Mary's resentment extends from the bitterness of having to do it all on her own. "I did a lot of things a lot of other girls didn't have to do because they started after me. The road was paved. So many of the other girls had someone to help them. Like Pinkie Smith, whose father is a trainer. Or some iron in the fire. I had none."

Pinkie Smith, on the other hand, asserts that she is a far superior rider to Mary, with or without a trainer father. "As far as I'm concerned," states Pinkie, "she can't even pack my tack."

At the Powder Puff Derby in Atlantic City last year—the most publicized of all the girls' races—Mary fought with Cheryl White, the only black female jockey.

"Cheryl let her mouth overload her ass" is how Mary sums up the situation. "She heard that I was named the favorite and she said, 'If Mary Bacon rides the favorite I'm going to put her over the rail.' When I heard what she said, I jumped all over her. She didn't get near me in the race."

Cheryl White refused to comment on the incident.

Part of Mary's resentment is a result of the long road she has traveled by herself, making her own way, and part of it can be assigned to temperament. Mary's mind is dedicated and determined; hers is a spit-and-do-it attitude. "If I could do anything in the world that I wanted to do," she once said, "I think I would get a sex transplant and reclaim the bug. Because I know I would be the leading bug rider in America."

The acid test of any jockey is how he reacts to a bad fall. After facing the very real possibility of death or of being crippled for life, some jockeys just cannot bring themselves to return to the track.

Mary Bacon has been hospitalized for three major accidents. Each has depressed her and made her obsessed with death, but she no sooner leaves the hospital than she's right back at the track. In 1970 she suffered a fractured vertebra when a two-year-old horse spooked at Waterford Park. In July, 1971, she broke her collarbone and several ribs, had collusions of the lung and went through the agony of a concussion at Ellis Park in Owensboro, Kentucky. After thirteen days in the Evansville hospital, Mary had had more than enough. "Pack the car!" she said to her agent. "We're going to Latonia!"

Judy packed the car, Mary sneaked out of the hospital and the two of them drove to Latonia Racetrack near Florence, Kentucky. Mary's shoulder was still in a cast. However, she sat in a hot tub to loosen the plaster, then removed it with a butcher knife.

September, 1972, at Pitt Park in Pennsylvania Mary had another serious fall. In the third race her mount, Tiger's Tune, clipped the heels of another horse and tossed Mary overboard. She landed on her head. She didn't move.

"We were going into the turn," Mary recalls, "and this kid was on the outside. He was just stupid. He crossed over the field and dropped right in front of me. And I went down.

He got a twenty-days' suspension, but he didn't do it on purpose. He's just dumb. He didn't look where he was going. That's how most spills happen. It's like a car accident. People don't look.

"I laid out on the racetrack and they thought I was dead." She remembers the occasion with considerable unhappiness. "They jerked my neck back and it looked like I snapped my head."

For a week Mary was in the intensive care unit. Four doctors, including a neurosurgeon, were in constant attendance.

During the first few days, before she regained consciousness, her mother sat by her bedside. Each morning a pleasant looking man would pop his head in the room and say hello.

"Who is that nice man?" Mary's mother finally asked the floor supervisor.

"He's the undertaker," she replied.

Whenever Mary can control the situation, which she couldn't do this time because she was unconscious, she insists on a female doctor. "As far as I'm concerned, men doctors are still men and they still read *Playboy* and all that. And I'm not going to have some man doctor come out to the racetrack and say, 'Hey, see that jockey over there? I had her on the table the other day, playing around with her."

It was finally determined that Mary had a severe concussion, and when she was released from the hospital 11 days later, she was advised to rest and take it easy.

The words were as wasted as any that one might use in telling Niagara Falls to slow down. Mary was soon back at the track, galloping horses and hustling mounts. "I got out of the hospital the eleventh day after the spill, and I rode that night," Mary says proudly. "I just signed a piece of paper saying it was all right for Mary Bacon to ride. The first horse I rode won, and the next horse won second. It got in the paper. And so the hospital called the track and said that I wasn't released, that I shouldn't ride. So I packed my tack and went to Kentucky. Just left the state and won three that week in Kentucky."

Mary is fascinated as well as mystified by the idea of death, very much like a matador who performs his ritual for the adulation of the cheering crowd. Mary's bravery is the ticket to the fame she seeks. And it's not at all clear in her own head. "I'm suicidal," she admits, "because I've had so many disappointments. I'll probably get killed on a horse."

After visiting Mary at the hospital, Johnny Bacon made up his mind that he had had enough. He'd been through so many spills himself, as well as so many accidents with Mary, that his patience was gone.

"I'm looking to get married again," he told Judy as Mary lay semiconscious in the hospital bed. "I'm not waiting around for her."

The following November Johnny did remarry, this time an eighteen-year-old country girl whom he had known for only three months. His young bride, Claudia Weaver, was—of all things—a jockey.

Johnny met Claudia at the Charles Town racetrack in West Virginia. She lived with her parents in a large farmhouse in the town and, like Mary, had grown up on horses. Their wedding, which took place at the finish line of the

Charles Town track, rivals only that of Tiny Tim to Miss Vicky on *The Tonight Show* as a candidate for the High Camp Hall of Fame.

A week before the wedding was to take place, the public relations department of the track ran an ad in several newspapers, inviting all lovers of racing to attend the gala event and promising each a slice of the newlyweds' 300-pound cake. Like many a smart society wedding, Claudia and Johnny's was to be an evening affair.

It was a motley group of race fans who crowded down close to the track the night of November 22 to watch the two jockeys promise to love and obey each other. Further, the night was bitterly cold, so the attire of the guests was more practical than fashionable. Most of the men wore down parkas or lumber jackets, while the women, some with their hair rolled in pink plastic curlers under babushkas, stood around in slacks and car coats.

As the heavy tones of the organ playing "Here Comes the Bride" pealed forth from the scattered loudspeakers, Claudia was paraded down the track in a horse-driven surrey with fringe on top. She looked radiant, dressed in a classic peau de soie gown with a full chapel train and a lace mantilla, as she took her place on the freshly constructed altar—a six-by-nine slab of plywood that had been covered with Astroturf and backed by a gigantic horseshoe, heavily layered with fugi mums.

While television cameras ground away and newspaper photographers surrounded the couple, the traditional Episcopalian service was read by the Reverend Temple Wheeler.

In the background was the whirring hum of a tractor, ready to perform its traditional between-races duty, harrowing the track. Funky, sensational weddings are not exactly a new thing to Reverend Wheeler. Some years ago he performed a similar service for a local baseball player, Kenneth Zombro, at home plate.

The bridesmaids, who stood alongside the altar, were dressed in lavender chiffon dresses, trailing in the dirt, with peek-a-boo sleeves. They wore net veils attached with lavishly looped bows, like Hallmark gift packages. Claudia's sister bit her lips to keep her teeth from chattering in the cold.

As the joyous couple placed rings on each other's fingers, the track announcer declared . . . "The results of the wedding are now official," and from the crowd erupted a raucous command, "Kiss da bride!"

The ceremony over, Claudia quickly swooped up the train of her gown and walked into the track building, where she rushed through candy wrappers, cardboard beer cups and popcorn containers on her way to the girl jockeys' quarters.

Slipping out of her bridal white, she pulled on a pair of wrinkled leotards and some slightly soiled socks that she had brought along in her overnight bag. Then she put on her riding helmet and silks.

"Johnny wears my clothes all the time and I wear his," she says, echoing the words of the woman in whose footsteps she was following.

To cap the evening, the newlyweds raced against each other in the seventh race; appropriately, it was a maiden claiming race named the "Mr. and Mrs. Purse." Johnny rode the show horse and Claudia finished sixth, out of the money.

Why did Johnny Bacon marry Claudia Weaver, if not for the simple fact of love? "I couldn't imagine myself married to a girl that I couldn't talk about racing with," Johnny said, sitting in the living room of the Weavers' house the day before the wedding. "On the other hand, I want Claudia to quit riding. It's too dangerous."

Claudia Bacon didn't protest too much. Like many of the girl jockeys, she prefers her racing on a part-time basis. "Now I can do it, like, for a hobby," she says. "But I'm thinkin' that I'd like to be a beautician. A lot of my girlfriends are doin' that and I always liked workin' on people's hair."

Johnny's wedding knocked the spunk out of Mary Bacon for a while and left her deeply depressed. Not only had he deserted her, he had publicly humiliated her as well. Ever since their divorce the preceding February, Mary had been telling everyone that the only reason they got the divorce was so they could ride together. "Johnny and I are as much in love as ever," Mary would tell reporters when they asked about her romantic life.

Sitting in the Compton Village Motor Inn opposite the Detroit Race Course just ten days after the wedding, Mary fought back tears as she talked. "Johnny doesn't love her. He just did this to get back at me."

Then the conversation turned to her daughter, Suzie. "I had the papers drawn up so that in the event of my death, Suzie will go to my sister in Los Angeles. That's what! So Johnny can't get her because I'll tell you what, that dumb no class broad that Johnny married is never even going to see Suzie Bacon! I'd take a gun and put it to her head and it wouldn't bother me in the least little bit. I wouldn't even blink an eye. And you know something? I could do it to Johnny, too. Because I love him and I hate him."

Mary may have lost this round, but she believes that she still has an ace or two up her sleeve. When *Playboy* asked her to pose nude, she jumped at the chance, knowing how furious Johnny would be when he saw her publicly displaying to millions of men the body he once loved. "I got to thinking about it, and I knew that when that nude came out in *Playboy*, well, I knew it would be hung up in the jocks' rooms. And that one of these days, Johnny was going to walk in and see a picture of me, sitting there half-naked, and just flip! He'll go rip it down, it will make him so mad."

At the same time, there is an ironic touch to Mary's posing and she sees the humor in the situation. "I look like a twelve-year-old kid without a bra on. I told the photographer, 'You'd better cut my head off and put it on someone else's body.'"

Mary believes that her posing will advance her career. She smiles when she thinks about it, and she hasn't smiled much recently. "The only time I smile anymore," she says, "is when I'm in the winner's circle. I've had a lot of spills and I know that I'm like a fighter. I'm not the same girl I was a few years ago."

There is no trace of humor when she talks about Johnny because she remembers too much, and her feelings about him are still divided. "I've always said that Johnny will be the death of me, and he probably will. I never was that way until he and I started having trouble." Then there is a pause. "Johnny can ride circles around me! He's the best!" And another pause. "He wanted to be the star. But he wasn't when I was around."

But if Mary still loves Johnny, she also still loves racing and horses. "I hide behind horses," Mary often admits. "When I'm on a horse, I'm queen. All these disappointments in my life have made me more obsessed with horses. Even the bad spills haven't stopped me. I've hidden further and further behind them." And though a sense of fatalism pervades, only momentarily does it surface. "I have no desire to live anymore. I won't live another year. I know I won't. They didn't think I would live after the last spill."

If Mary Bacon is achieving her goal, she knows what it has cost her, what she has had to do to get where she is. "I wanted it so bad," she says. "I had to take a lot of dishonest and bad routes to get it. There are a lot of things I had to do that I'm ashamed I had to do to ride winners."

The first Christmas without Johnny was a rough one for Mary. Now that he is married again, he seems to have forgotten not only Mary but the small daughter who looks just like him.

At Christmas, Mary was riding at Fairgrounds in New Orleans. "I guess that I'm just like every other mother. Suzie says that her daddy doesn't love her anymore, and I don't have the guts to tell her that she's right. On Christmas, every time the phone would ring, Suzie would run to it and yell, 'Daddy! Daddy!' And it wasn't him. He didn't even bother to call her. He didn't even call his mother. This girl that he married, I think she was afraid he might send Suzie a ten-dollar present. Suzie waited in the jocks' room where I was racing. We waited all day and he didn't call, so we went home and she cried herself to sleep.

"And then on her birthday, March 4, she was four years old. Days ahead, every time the mailman came, Suzie thought that he was going to bring her a present from her daddy. Well, nothing ever came. And she said to me, 'Daddy doesn't love me anymore.' And I said, 'No, it probably just got lost in the mail.' So I went out and bought something and signed his name to it and mailed it myself."

Some good luck came Mary's way last year in the person of Jack Van Berg, the top owner-trainer in the nation. Mary had been riding for him for several years, and he decided that she was ready for Aqueduct.

In the meantime, Johnny was racing at Waterford Park. "It's a cheap track," Mary explains. "They run a $1200 horse, where at Aqueduct they're going to run a $12,000 one. I was looking through *The Racing Form* one day and glanced at the Waterford entries and noticed that Johnny Bacon was there, and I nearly died laughing. I was sitting in the jocks' room at Aqueduct. As soon as I got done riding, I went to a stationery store and bought a card. On the outside it said 'My Deepest Sympathy Is With You.' It was the kind you would send when there's a death in the family. On the inside it said something about comforting you in your time of deepest sorrow. And I cut out the Waterford entries and underlined Waterford in red ink and circled Johnny's name. Then I cut out the Aqueduct entries and circled my own name."

The Big A has not been exactly overwhelmed with Mary. The track has been Robyn Smith's turf for three years, but Mary's fighting spirit has returned and she is determined to leave her mark. During Mary's first week there, a man in the grandstand said to her, "You might be queen of the bullrings and Van Berg might be king of the gyps, but you're in New York now." Typically, Mary was not nonplussed. Turning to the man, she replied quietly: "You know what? New York's going to think they're Detroit when we get through with them!"

2

Railbird to Jockey Joan O'Shea, after she lost a race:
"Go home where you belong and cook dinner!"
Joan O'Shea: "I can't cook, either."

Any female jockey worth her stirrups is an odd duck. It requires so much grit and sheer guts to swing a leg over a half-ton horse and ride against a pack of brusque little men that ordinary women, most of whom fit neatly into stereotypes, just don't cut the mustard. There are now approximately sixty women who have jockey licenses in the United States, but the majority of them ride infrequently, and when they do, it is usually at the rinky-dink tracks that run broken-down nags on a one-way trip to the glue factory.

Most of the girls who earn their license soon learn that owners are reluctant to put a fragile female on an animal that on the average represents a $6000 investment. Some women are frightened away by their first spill or accident. After a serious fall, only a remarkably brave person will return to the track with the same daring that was displayed before hospitalization. A girl rider in Maryland was on her third mount when the horse flipped over and broke her back.

She was paralyzed for five months, and never raced again.

The small band of women who support themselves as jockeys are fascinating flukes, to be sure, but they are more than mere curiosities. Tough, street-smart, often ruthless, they can be just as cunning as Becky Sharp and nervier than Jesse James.

Robyn Smith, the top woman rider in America, has had an outlandish life by anybody's yardstick. Two and a half years ago, with only three winning races to her credit, Robyn started banging on barn doors at Belmont, the toughest track in the country, begging trainers for mounts. Now she is a full-fledged member of the elite jockey colony at the Big A, where she competes against such luminaries as Baeza, Velasquez and Cordero, often carrying the famed cerise and white diamond silks of millionaire Alfred Gwynne Vanderbilt.

Even though she has earned and won the plaudits of her peers and her fans, Robyn holds herself at a distance, purposely, it seems, shrouding her life with an aura of mystery. In New York racing circles, she is known as the "Jackie-O of the backstretch—without the money."

Like Fitzgerald's Gatsby, Robyn created a glamorous history for herself. She claimed at one time to be the daughter of a wealthy lumberman and to have been raised in Hawaii and educated at Stanford, a B.A. in English, Class of '66. After that charade, it was a brief career in the movies. "I became acting-conscious while I was at school," she told reporters, "and decided I'd like to take a crack at it. M-G-M gave me a contract."

The real scenario of Robyn Smith's life is a most unhappy story. It is no surprise that she might try to bury it.

Instead of growing up in Hawaii, she spent years in foster homes in Portland, Oregon. Her real father, who drove a Yellow cab, divorced her mother when Robyn was only two. He never tried to see his daughter again.

Robyn's mother, Constance Miller, is a plump, soft-spoken woman who says she's been married four times, once to a man who's been married ten times. When young she was a Hollywood extra, where she usually played in nightclub acts and harem scenes. Now in her early sixties, Mrs. Miller works off and on as a typist, a PBX operator or a practical nurse in the San Francisco area.

Robyn tells everyone that her parents are dead, although her mother would like to establish contact with her runaway daughter.

"I'd like to send you something real beautiful," Mrs. Miller wrote to her daughter last Christmas while Robyn was racing at Aqueduct. But she did not receive a reply.

"Robyn's living in a fantasy world," Mrs. Miller says, adding with unmaternal candor that truthfulness was never one of Robyn's strong traits.

The most intriguing aspect of Robyn Smith is not her storytelling ability but her natural talent as a rider. While Robyn was going to acting school—she never actually had a contract with M-G-M—a boy she was dating had a horse with trainer Bruce Headley at Santa Anita, and Robyn went out to watch it work one morning.

"I saw a girl galloping a horse and couldn't believe my eyes," Robyn told a reporter. "It never dawned on me women could be a part of racing. I've always had a tremendous affinity for animals of all kinds, and I really got excited about the possibility of working at the racetrack. I asked Bruce if he needed an exercise girl—I think I told him I'd been riding for years, which I hadn't—but he didn't need anybody at the time. It was almost a year later that he offered me a job galloping horses."

Now Robyn is booting home winners at Aqueduct, the Taj Mahal of American racing.

Patty Barton, who races at Waterford Park in West Virginia, is another maverick who, on her own, decided that she was going to make a mark in thoroughbred racing.

Nature aided her by giving her a body strong enough to kick sand in the face of the late Charles Atlas. Her compact rear end is totally devoid of the soft upholstery usually found among the feminine gender. Her rib cage is set wide like a man's and doesn't allow for a waist. Up her arms and across her shoulders, muscles bulge in every direction and actually ripple when she moves the upper part of her body.

"I'd place better in a Mr. America contest than in a Miss America," Patty laughed while stripping to get into her riding silks one evening. "I'm the only mother I know whose kids bring the neighbors in to look at her muscles." Yet Lee Arthur, a sportscaster for KDKA-TV in Pittsburgh, once remarked after interviewing Patty: "There's a beauty about Patty Barton. She has tremendous charm and a personality which radiates."

Like Mary Bacon and Robyn Smith, Patty's early years were also bleak. She bailed out as quickly as she could.

Patty never knew her real parents. She was adopted from the New York Foundling Home by a factory worker and his wife. The family had its heart set, of course, on bringing up a soft little girl whom they could shower with dolls and dress up in pretty frocks with ribbons.

"I can remember one time my grandmother asked me what I wanted to be when I grew up," Patty says. "I said 'Gene Autry.' She took me in the bathroom and washed my mouth out with soap."

A natural rebel, Patty ignored her family and spent all her free time hanging around horses near her home on the outskirts of Miami. "Whenever I came home from the stables, I had to change my clothes outside before they would let me in the house," she remembers.

As soon as she was graduated from high school, Patty hired herself out to the IXL Ranch Show. "I used to ride bulls and broncs. Anything they'd put me on." The pay was poor, but she skimped by living in cheap boarding houses and existing on a diet of soda pop and bologna sandwiches. Between shows, she supplemented her income by driving a truck.

After six months of rodeoing, Patty married a cowboy, only to discover that in real life Lone Rangers aren't very romantic. "They all have those snap-button shirts, pressed and creased Levis and big hats—but every one of them has dirty underwear on underneath."

The Bartons had three children, but the marriage was not a good one. Charlie was a drinker, according to Patty, and when he was on the sauce she had to keep a loaded shotgun

"I'm just a little ol' cowgirl," says Mary Bacon who raced Appaloosas at Oklahoma bush tracks when she was only nine years old. Now twenty-five, Mary is one of the top women jockeys in America.—*Frank Methe*

Dressed in her racing outfit, Mary adjusts her helmet before facing the competition. "I even sleep in racing silks," claims the pretty blond, "seein' as I don't have any nightgowns."—*UPI*

"Some women shell out twenty-five bucks for a mud pack and I get 'em for free," quips Mary as she whips layers of sandy glop from her face after riding in the rain at Aqueduct.—*N.Y. Daily News*

Jockey Johnny Bacon, Mary's former husband, weds jockette Claudia Weaver on the Charles Town track between races. After the ceremony, the newlyweds switched into their silks and competed against each other in the seventh race.

—*Washington Star News*

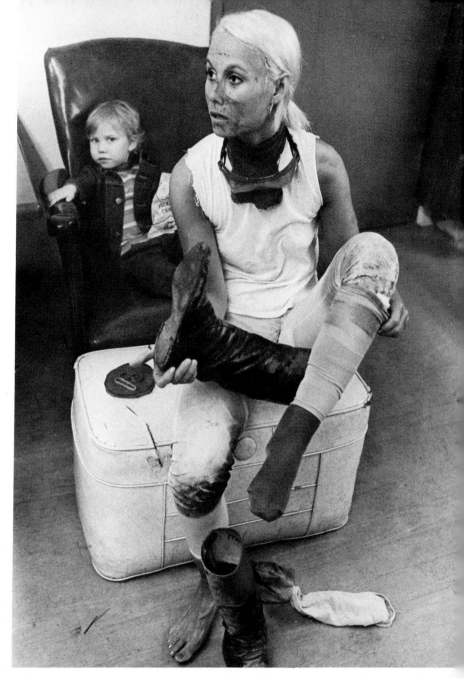

Exhausted from an afternoon of racing, Mary pulls off her boots while daughter Suzie looks on. "Suzie's not going to be a jockey if I have anything to do with it," Mary says. "Racing's much too rough for a woman."
—*Fred Smith*

Robyn Smith, the only woman to mount a sustained invasion of New York thoroughbred racing, cracked the Big A by begging mounts from the country's top trainers, some of whom quickly realized that the beautiful apprentice had genuine riding talent.—*Jim Raftery*

Diane Crump, who made thoroughbred racing history on February 7, 1969, when she became the first woman to ride a major track, is shown charging down the stretch in her second race, on Bridle 'n Bit. —*UPI*

Dazed after a spill at Gulfstream Park, Diane Crump rests in the track's first aid room.—*Jim Raftery*

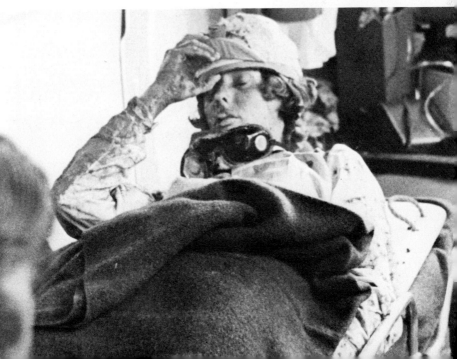

Barbara Jo weighing in at Aqueduct for the first time. Later that afternoon, with pigtails flying, she outrode the competition by two lengths aboard an untried 13–1 shot named Bravy Galaxy.—*Wide World*

The first woman to win against men at a major American sport, Barbara Jo Rubin is all smiles as she is kissed by male jockeys Herberto Arroyo, left, and Craig Perret, right, in front of her trailer dressing room at Tropical Park in Miami. Barbara Jo won seven of her first ten races, an amazing record.—*Wide World*

Tropical PARK
JOCKEY ROOM
(GIRL JOCKEY'S ONLY)
Courtesy BOB WILMATH

Patty Barton used to earn $1 an hour tending bar. Now she makes up to $500 a night, as the winningest female jockey in the nation. Patty races year round at Waterford Park, West Virginia, where the competition isn't stiff and the chances to ride are plentiful.—*UPI*

Sandy Schleiffers, the first woman admitted to the Jockey's Guild, came to the racetrack from the Sisters of St. Francis convent in Clinton, Iowa. Although she loves racing, she hopes someday to resume her religious career. —*Jim Raftery*

Left: Daughter of owner–trainer Walt Peltier, Violet "Pinkie" Smith had a head start on becoming a jockey. "Even though I got my dad helping me, it ain't no picnic out there," Pinkie says.

Jennifer Rowland, Maryland's leading woman jockey, gets last-minute instructions from her trainer prior to the start of the all-girl "My Fair Lady Handicap" at Laurel Racetrack.—*Washington Star-News*

Donna Hillman, 5 feet 4½ inches, 104 pounds, enjoys Indian wrestling men twice her size. "I'm stronger than any guy I know," claims the pretty jockey who once modeled for *Harper's Bazaar*.—*UPI*

After capturing first place at Laurel's "My Fair Lady Handicap," Donna pats her lucky mount, Jolly Fox. "I don't like riding with all girls," she says. "I'd much rather be one of the regular guys."—*Washington Star-News*

Donna Hillman charges down the homestretch at Laurel trailed by Diane Heiss, a St. Louis debutante who traded tea dances for riding stirrups.—*Washington Star News*

Judy Barrett listens attentively while her trainer, Don LeVine, explains how he wants her to handle the reins on an upcoming mount. The daughter of a British pub owner, Judy came to the United States hoping to make it big on the American turf.—*Jim Raftery*

Judy gets a leg up from Don LeVine as she mounts Sunny Day Girl at Hialeah, Florida.—*Jim Raftery*

Left: Diane Crump and Mary Bacon reminisce before the "Boots and Bows" all-girl race at Atlantic City. "We're the veterans," says Mary. "We've been through the wars together."—*Jim Raftery*

The fourteen participants in the "Boots and Bows" handicap line up before the Atlantic City race held on August 28, 1972. The most successful of the "Powder Puff" derbies, this one always draws a large crowd.—*Jim Raftery*

Mary "Mike" Ryan, a former steeplechase jockey, chats with her boss Johnny Campo, one of the nation's top trainers. As Campo's assistant, Mike holds the most important position of any woman training thoroughbreds in America. "He trusts me with a million dollars worth of stock," Mike says.—*Jim Raftery*

Calder's bugler, Prina, calls the horses onto the Florida track. An Israeli citizen, Prina attended the Juilliard School of Music and has played with symphonies.—*UPI*

Jubilant after winning the "Boots and Bows," Cheryl White, the only black woman jockey in the nation, triumphantly holds her whip in the air. Horses have been a big thing in Cheryl's life for as long as she can remember. Her father is a trainer and the family owns nine race horses.—*Jim Raftery*

As agent for jockey Rocky Gabrial, Francine Plotnick solicits mounts for her client. "It's like being a theatrical agent," Francine says. "You really have to get out and hustle if you are going to make any money."—*Jim Raftery*

by the door of their shack in Alamogordo, New Mexico, because she was tired of sitting up with him all night for fear that he might fall asleep with a lighted cigarette in his hand and burn down the shack.

"Charlie ran off with my best friend," Patty says bitterly. "At least, I thought she was my best friend." In order to support her three children and herself, Patty galloped horses in the morning and worked as a cocktail waitress at night.

"So many girls wanted to be jockeys for the glory. But I didn't want to have to work so damned hard. They were only paying me a dollar a head to exercise horses, and I figured I could make that in one race as a jockey."

Patty believes that a woman jockey has to let the male riders know that she means business or else they'll mow her over.

Once a jockey named Randy bumped into her on purpose when they were coming down the backstretch at Waterford Park. Patty lost no time. As soon as the jocks filed back into their quarters after the race, she knocked him against the wall.

They fell to the floor, where Randy pulled Patty's hair and Patty yanked Randy's genitals. "A fight is a fight," she explains. "It means hurt the other guy before he hurts you."

After the fight broke up, Randy snickered, "That's the closest she's been to a man in a long time."

"You go tell that little so-and-so that there was hardly anything to get hold of," Patty told her valet.

❖   ❖   ❖

Of all the women jockeys, Sandy Schleiffers is probably the most unusual. Watching this four-foot-eleven spitfire with a cute, little boy's face chug-a-lug Canadian Clubs with the male jocks, or hearing her cuss out a trainer who's taken her off a horse she's been riding regularly, it is hard to believe that she spent two years in a convent and plans one day to return to the cloistered life. At the track they call her the flying nun.

Asked to compare her racing life to the nunnery, Sandy paused a moment, then said, "I think the convent is probably a hell of a lot rougher. In the convent everybody lives closely together and so you really have to have a lot of patience."

Sandy didn't care much for wearing a religious habit. In fact, the only time she's had a skirt on since leaving the convent was when she had to keep an appointment with the head of a monastery in Youngstown, Ohio. "He said he wouldn't take me out to dinner if I didn't put a skirt on," she recalls.

Sandy was raised on a farm outside Seattle, and almost from infancy she excelled as a rider. When she was only five years old she was breaking yearlings, according to her proud mother.

As a jockey, Sandy has distinguished herself on several fronts. She was the first woman deemed worthy to become a member of the Jockeys Guild, and she was one of the first women ever to be subpoenaed by a federal grand jury on a charge of race-fixing. The accusation, which was never proved, was brought against her at the Finger Lakes track by an envious girl rider who had not been getting many mounts.

On the night of her twenty-sixth birthday last November, Sandy went to a night spot in Meadowlands, West Virginia, with some of her friends who wanted to take her out to celebrate. Dressed in cowboy boots, dusty Levis and a faded Western shirt, Sandy moseyed up to the bar and told the waitress, "The drinks are on me."

As the party carried on into the night, Sandy decided to call her grandmother in California. Caressing the receiver of the pay phone next to the garish neon-lit fountain in the entrance of the bar, her voice changed from its harsh locker room toughness to a frail, little-girl tone that suddenly seemed so much younger than twenty-six, and much too sweet and vulnerable for a jockey.

"Grandma! Grandma, it's me! Sandy! Don't you remember? It's my birthday. I thought you were going to call me today. Ohhh, Grandma, how could you forget?"

When she returned to the table, she looked as if she were going to cry.

Religion still plays a big part in Sandy's life. On her racing sweatshirts, which the jockeys wear under their silks on cold days, Sandy has taped JMJ. In Catholic grade schools the children often initial their paperwork with these letters as a good luck prayer. In the same spirit, Sandy makes the sign of the cross just before breaking from the gate.

There is no such animal as a "typical" girl jockey. Identical twins Linda Richmond and Lois Meals, who both race for a living, are the daughters of Pittsburgh school-teachers. Apprentice rider Diane Heiss is a former debutante from St. Louis. Donna Hillman, who modeled for *Harper's Bazaar*, is the daughter of actress Joan Barkley, who appeared with Clark Gable. Lottie Von Brommssen is a Pan Am stewardess who moonlights as a jockey at foreign tracks during her stopoffs around the world.

And not all female jockeys are young. Arline Ditmore is thirty-six; Joan O'Shea is forty-seven. Lillian Jenkins, dubbed the "wild woman of the bush tracks," is in her sixties. Last year one of her horses broke loose and ran smack into a car that was parked in a nearby lot. The car was demolished, but Mrs. Jenkins was back riding three weeks later.

When girls first began to ride, most racetrackers wondered about the number of women who would muster up enough courage to apply for a jockey's license. They were concerned, too, about the possible attitudes and actions of the men who held their licenses. Were the women to be main-show performers, top-flight attractions, or were they to be sideshow freaks? No one knew the answers, but nearly everyone had an opinion.

Some track officials predicted that within ten years every other rider out of the gate would be a girl. In this advanced spirit, Calder built a $50,000 women's jockey quarters, only to have it remain basically idle, thus far, because so few girls race there. The space has been put to other uses, and the girls are now relegated to a small dressing room.

Other knowledgeable observers of the equine scene dismissed women as hothouse flowers, destined to fade once they lose the spotlight and were not guaranteed good horses.

Now, four years later, neither prediction has proved precisely correct. What's happened is that a small, but increasing, number of women have their licenses, while the number of those willing to take on the less glamorous jobs at the track is growing every day. There is a proved market for them.

The United States has 138 racecourses and forty-five million paying customers a year. Another fact surprising to most people is that horse racing attracts twice as many spectators as major football games. The number of tracks in the country has nearly doubled since 1954, and tracks are now found in almost every state, extending from Scarborough Downs in Maine and Suffolk Downs in Massachusetts to Longacres and Sundown Park in Washington, from Del Mar in southern California to Tropical Park in Miami.

Home-grown jocks (i.e., American) are bound up in a biological fact—they are simply getting bigger year by year. Youngsters today are larger than their parents. So the market is forcing the American male out of the picture, leaving it wide open for women and foreigners. Whether he accepts the fact or not, the local male jockey, like the American buffalo, is a vanishing breed.

Robyn Smith finished seventh in the jockey standings at the 1972 Aqueduct spring meeting. She had only ninety-eight mounts. Except for one other jockey at the Big A, every other jockey there had twice as many mounts as Robyn. Angel Cordero was the only jock with a better percentage of wins than Robyn's 20 percent. But even more impressive to note, according to an article in *Sports Illustrated*, is that "at the top track in the country she was the leading U.S. jockey; the six riders ranked ahead of her were foreigners. By the end of the meeting, it could be fairly argued that the best young American jockey was a woman."

There is still a tremendous amount of pressure and prejudice against women riders in spite of the fact that licenses are now being given more easily to those who are qualified. If you ask a trainer such as Preston King why he is reluctant to place women on his horses, he will parrot the sentiments of many of his colleagues. Standing in the racing secretary's office at Aqueduct, he offered this precise evaluation: "A 112-pound girl and a 112-pound man are not equal in strength. Women just don't have it in the pectoral muscles, which is where you need it when you're riding. As a result, women are often weak finishers in the last fifty to sixty yards."

Well, that might be true for many women. But aren't there any exceptions?

"Robyn's probably the best of the girl riders," says King. "She's not a Shoemaker or a Baltzhazer, but she's not bad. I'd say, on a ten-point scale, Robyn's about a seven."

Some trainers believe that the very qualities that make women such good exercise riders will work against them as jockeys. The lightness and the gentle touch which are so effective early in the morning, they say, will likely make it difficult to control mounts in a race.

Many of the women jockeys state that no matter what they do or what they accomplish, men will continue to put them down. Arline Ditmore summed up the attitude of many: "If you win, it's dumb luck. If you get beaten, it's, 'Look at that fool girl. She blew the race.' "

Just as some people tend to lump all blacks together, the same thing happens with the girl riders. A racetrack fan once walked up to Barbara Jo Rubin and said in an angry voice, "I lost twenty bucks on you in Chicago last year."

"I never raced in Chicago," Barbara Jo retorted.

Some of the girls become so fed up with the simple prejudice that they'd like to pass themselves off as boys. Jennifer Rowland, the top girl bug rider in Maryland, said, "I have thought of arriving at a strange track and pretending I was a boy." One day after racing at Pimlico in Baltimore, Jennifer was driving to Charles Town when her car broke down. It was evening, and she was afraid to hitchhike as a woman, so she tucked her hair in her cap and, with no makeup on and her slender body, passed as a boy. When a truck driver picked her up and he turned out to be all right, she flipped off her hat and let her long hair fall to her shoulders, to the amazement of the trucker. "Listen," she said, "could you hurry it up? I've got to make the first race at Charles Town."

As a general rule, male jockeys are only too pleased to keep alive the idea that women just don't have what it takes to be good riders. Obviously, it's to their economic advantage to keep women down.

Jockeys are among the highest paid members of the sporting fraternity. The top dozen jocks earn an average of $200,-000 a year, and most of this comes from their 10 percent of the winnings in races with big stakes, and the number of these races has skyrocketed in recent years.

Only 10 percent of all jockeys make the winner's circle and the headlines with any regularity. There is obviously a great difference between the salary of a Hartack, who averages 1000 mounts a year and earns as much as a movie star, and a jock at some track in Dismal Seepage, Illinois, or in North Overshoe, Idaho, who averages—if he's lucky—250 mounts and earns a salary in the $6000 to $7000 range. There is even more disparity here when one considers that some of the girls are not averaging the same number of mounts as the boy who is on the other end of the scale from Hartack; their salaries are often considerably less than $6000.

Everybody knows that a jockey is supposed to be a fireball, a real bombshell: super-alert, at-the-ready, recklessly brave and tough to the grainy marrow of his bones. So, one might ask, if a woman can do it, how can it be so hard?

Arline Ditmore, who races at Aqueduct, remembers that after she won a race one day, another jockey got off his horse and threw his hands in the air in a Joblike gesture of despair. "Arline Ditmore beat me! Arline Ditmore beat me!" He moaned as though some whimsical god had subjected him to the lowest level of hell.

Added to any problems a jockey might have about his Lilliputian size is the burden of possessing little education. The average rider comes from a poor or middle-class family. He completed grade school and went on to high school for a few years. Chances are better than average that he did not graduate. Given these disadvantages, the stereotype of the jockey image often bears itself in real life. Jocks are big tippers; many carry their money around in a gambler's roll. The flashy Western clothing and the big cars are a trademark with many.

When girls first started to ride, many jockeys claimed that they were psychologically incapable of competing against females for fear that they might injure them. In practice, the women report that the men are much tougher on them than they are on their male counterparts.

If a girl reports an incident to a steward, she is much more likely to be tagged a squealer than is a man who files. Barbara Jo Rubin, who has since retired from racing, recalls that one foggy night at Waterford Park she was riding a horse named Cohesion, and just as she moved into the lead, the jockey next to her took his whip and whacked her across the back.

"At first I thought, What the shit is this?" she recalls. "Well, I decided it was just an accident. Then he hit me again, and then he pops my horse right on the head. I wanted to reach over and knock him off his horse, but I figured if I did, the stewards would catch it on the film patrol and take my number down, and I wouldn't get any purse or anything.

"So then I figured, I'll fix him. So I rode up to him and gave him the biggest smile, and he almost fell off his horse. And I went on and won by eight or nine lengths.

"The stewards knew there was something funny in that race, and they came down afterward and one of them asked, 'My God, what happened?'

" 'Nothing happened,' I said."

On the other hand, there are advantages that a woman racer has over her male opponent. If a jockey is suspected of carrying a buzzer, he will actually be frisked by the stewards. "They wouldn't dare touch me," laughs one girl jockey as she tucks a buzzer up her sleeve just before a race.

At the beginning of the girl jockey craze, many owners and trainers tried to cash in on the phenomenon for its publicity value. But now, five years later, most girl jockeys can't even retain an agent, yet still they refuse to give up and go out and hustle mounts for themselves. Making the rounds from barn to barn, pleading with trainers to put them on horses, can be a humiliating experience, much like an actor who auditions and is turned down for a part: "Don't call us . . . we'll call you." "You can't just sit in the tack room on your ass and expect to get mounts," says Cheryl White, expressing the attitude of most of the girls.

Even Kathy Kusner is finding things difficult five years after her now-historic lawsuit. While she is without doubt one of the two or three leading women riders in the world, it has been said by one trainer, "Kusner can't buy a mount on this circuit." Part of her problem is that she was basically trained as a show rider and she has not been fully able to adapt, or switch, her style.

Regardless of a person's potential ability, what it all comes down to is that a jockey can't win races unless he or she gets winning mounts. "Horses make jockeys, jockeys don't make horses" is a cliché on the racetrack. And, as with most clichés, there is a simple truth hiding within. The jock who gets the most mounts has a better chance of winning races, which in turn helps him get more good mounts. The records of the famous jockeys—Shoemaker, Hartack, Arcaro—bear this out.

Even with all the advances made by the women's liberation movement, there are still many men who feel reluctant about putting a woman in a position where she might be injured. Although film patrols eliminate most of the rough riding of former years, and the introduction of the Caliente helmet has reduced the element of danger on the track, the mortality rate among jockeys in action is still higher than practically any other group of athletes.

Joe Gottstein, the former president of Longacres Racetrack, once told jockey Pinkie Smith, whom he has known since she was a child, "I've picked up many a boy off that racetrack and some of them have been dead in my arms. I'd sure hate to think I'd ever have to pick you up."

In order to dispel any illusions that trainers cherish about women belonging to the weaker sex, many female jockeys exercise "female machismo"—they ape all the roughneck mannerisms of the boys, often to an exaggerated extent.

Donna Hillman weighs only 104 pounds, but she regularly challenges men twice her size to Indian wrestling contests. And she often wins. Last year Donna did a television commercial for Clairol in which she gets off a horse and shakes her blonde hair. But she found that her lovely golden locks were not advancing her career as a jockey.

"Everybody used to comment on my pretty hair," she says. "It was just what I didn't want. So I figured if I cut my hair off and arm-wrestled a few people, maybe they'd get the idea I was strong and can ride." Then she adds, somewhat wistfully, "If I could be a boy for two years, I'd be one of the leading riders in the country."

Lois Meals builds up her strength by gulping down the same liquid vitamins that she feeds to the horses that her husband trains. And Jennifer Rowland eats flax seeds, which are given to horses to make their coat bloom.

Most of the male jockeys are stronger, however, so the women are entering the situation at a natural disadvantage. And even with all the display of female machismo, the racetrack remains a citadel where chivalry is relatively unknown. Women jockeys do have the passport to success—their talent and their license—but they must still beg for the opportunity.

One girl remembers with a sardonic laugh that she had been asked to write an article for a leading racing magazine on the subject of girl jockeys. "Of course, I didn't tell them what it was really like," she says. "How trainers are always trying to screw you. I didn't tell them how, when they're puttin' you on a horse, they try to pinch your tit or grab your ass. But the whole trouble is that you can't say anything or they won't put you on their horses. You just have to be nice and try to ignore it. Or laugh it off.

"I remember one time in Ohio a trainer was supposed to be giving me a leg-up on my horse in the paddock and his hand slipped into my crotch. When I looked at him, he just pretended like it was an accident. Well, I went on and won the race. So the next day he was helping me up on another horse and I said sarcastically, 'If you give me another leg-up like you did yesterday, I might make it to the Derby.'"

Not only does a girl jockey face the problem of being regarded more as a potential source of erotic delight than as a serious rider by the men on the track, but she must also suffer their jealous wives. One trainer said to Linda Richmond, "My wife would have a conniption if I let you ride."

Last fall, Charles Town decided to include within their new $100,000 jockey quarters a recreational facility that could be used by both the male and the female jockeys. Leading off from this common room would be separate dressing rooms for each. When the male jockeys' wives heard about this, they protested that such a setup would enable the girls to peek at their husbands in various states of undress.

According to Claudia Weaver, who was racing at Charles Town at the time, the woman who headed up this rebellion wasn't exactly married to the Burt Reynolds of the Jockeys Guild. "He looks like he's been run through a cornfield on his head," Claudia said.

Claudia was sitting in the racing secretary's office the day the wives came to inspect the famous dressing room. "You're not changing up there," the leader of the delegation told her. "It's nothing but a whorehouse."

"Want to see my jockey's license?" Claudia replied. "I have every right to be up there if that's where I'm supposed to change."

Later she added, "If those jockeys were any kind of men at all, they would have spanked their women and told them to go home where they belonged."

The result of it all was that the jockeys decided by ballot to let the girls stay, and the track officials agreed to seal up one door that the wives found especially objectionable.

At most tracks the girls change in the first-aid room, and at a number of these they must then go to the men's quarters to be weighed in. Rather than welcoming members of the opposite sex, some jockeys regard this as an invasion of their inviolate domain.

Bill Hartack, who rides regularly at Calder in Miami, sat in the comfortable home of his friend George Stidham and talked about the locker room dilemma. "At Calder the main scale you have to check on is in the male jocks' room. I walk around the jocks' room naked all the time, and, boy, they got me shellshocked. You see, I hit the box a lot [the steam bath] because I have to reduce a lot, and you don't reduce with your clothes on. So I'll come out of the box to take a break or to have a cigarette, and some girl will be standing there, ready to weigh in."

When Hartack's comments were repeated to a female jockey who races regularly at Calder, she seemed truly unaware that her presence had upset him. "Oh, I never notice faces," she said.

Perhaps the only real advantage that women jockeys have over men is that it sometimes is easier for them to meet the required weight stipulation. But just like some of the men, some of the women are also forced to live on a diet of steak and eggs every day in order to make weight. Even a glass of water can push them beyond the weight limit.

It is not unusual around racetracks to hear tales, often fanciful, about jockeys and their weights. Of starved riders leaping from a horse to run to the infield, where they fall on their knees and eat the grass. Or jockeys so faint with hunger they can barely mount their horse.

A woman must thus sacrifice the big things—cake, fried foods, candy, liquor. And she must also give up the little things. So for twenty-four hours a day she may have a monkey on her back. Often she can't even chew gum because gum might make her thirsty, and liquids add weight. Jocks are known to devour entire boxes of Ex-lax—one of the best ways to lose weight quickly and ruin the insides at the same time. Forced heaving is not uncommon.

One reason Barbara Jo Rubin quit racing was that she literally ate herself out of a job. Another is that she broke her pelvis and, for her, riding is still a painful experience.

"Barbara Jo's the kind of girl who'd be making brownies and the directions would say thirty minutes. She'd take them out at twenty minutes because she couldn't wait," Linda Richmond says. To which Barbara Jo retorts: "That's not true. I'd eat the batter."

Barbara, like most jockeys, often resorted to heaving for instantaneous weight loss when she was riding. "I'd go out and eat six pounds of food in an hour and a half," Barbara Jo admits. "I'd figure I'll have to heave it and I'd heave about an ounce and end up six pounds heavier."

While Barbara Jo was racing at Liberty Bell, the jockeys volunteered to wear shorts so she could use the steam box. But the management vetoed the idea.

So Barbara Jo tried to lose weight as she traveled in her car from track to track. "I'd wrap myself in Saran Wrap and I'd put on pants and a shirt. Then I'd put on jackets and gloves. Get in the car and start driving. Turn the heater up. . . . This would be when the weather was maybe ninety degrees. I had to have gloves on because the steering wheel would burn my hands. Then I started passing out too much and almost wrecked my car a few times and I had to stop doing that."

The women jockeys retain their independence to a remarkable degree, and they continue their struggle for mounts and equal pay and equal opportunities, but most of them don't want to have anything to do with the women's lib movement. For one thing, they don't understand many of the philosophical issues that give the movement its impetus; for another, they already have much more freedom than most of the women they know.

A comment from one is fairly typical of the reaction of all: "I don't like the movement. I think it's stupid. They make a big issue out of things that aren't necessary to make a big issue out of. I mean, as far as women having the same job opportunities and the same rights . . . like maybe there might be a tavern down the street that they won't allow a woman in or something of this nature. That's fine. But when they come down to a man can't open a door for a lady, or you can't have *men* or *women* on a restroom, because they call that discrimination. And all this kind of garbage. Burning their bras out in Pershing Square or wherever the hell it was . . . that's asinine, completely asinine."

And another offers the following when asked how to advise a girl on whether to become a jockey: "Don't! Not unless she can put up with the good times and bad times and put up with some pretty ratty people and some good people. And a life that you don't know if you are going to have food in your mouth one minute and a big party the next. You don't know who's going to be stabbing you in the back and you don't know who's going to be your friend. And if you can't hack that, then don't do it."

For Cheryl White, a black jockey, riding isn't so base. "I enjoy it because it doesn't have the problems of a more normal life. On a racetrack it's more like one big, happy family. You don't find too many racial problems, and if you need money, you will always find someone who will give it to you."

3

Joe Garagiola: "Do girl jockeys wear jock straps?"
Barbara Jo: "No. We only wear what's necessary."

To look at her now, you would never guess that four years ago Barbara Jo Rubin stood the racing world on its ear.

In appearance, there is nothing left of Barbara Jo the jockey. The pigtailed, flat-chested teenager from Miami is now a shapely young woman—her full breasts cantilever beneath her blouse; her bottom is round but firm; and her long, shapely legs look as if they belong to a Las Vegas showgirl rather than a professional race rider. The rich, black hair that once hung from her racing helmet like two stalks of asparagus now flows freely over her shoulders and down her back. Her skin is soft, completely void of the leather-tough texture that is the trademark of a jockey. Only the eyes show her pain. The twinkling sapphires that used to shine with trust from the pages of newspapers and magazines are sadder and more guarded now.

"Not a girl in the world lived as fast as she did," says Brian Webb, her trainer, when speaking of Barbara Jo's spectacular rise to instant fame and her subsequent fall to relative obscurity.

Barbara Jo was the first female jockey to hit the big time. A month and a half after the Florida Racing Commission gave her a license, she cracked the sex barrier on pari-mutuel racetracks by romping a horse named Cohesion to a 6½-furlong victory at Charles Town. She thus became the first woman in American history to defeat the opposite sex in a major sporting contest.

After her Charles Town triumph, Barbara Jo set an incredible pace. She won seven of her first ten races, a record unparalleled in racing annals. Eddie Arcaro rode in 100 races before he got even one win.

The media went wild. Barbara Jo's picture was splashed on the front page of *The Daily News*. Ed Sullivan paid her $1500 to appear on his television show. She did a skit with Lena Horne on *The Kraft Music Hall* and later traded quips with *The Today Show*'s Joe Garagiola.

Barbara Jo Rubin, the jockey, quickly became a road show. Her trainer and her agent booked her for one-night stands at tracks up and down the East coast, which happily forked out $1000 to $1500 just to have Barbara Jo make an appearance, regardless of whether she won. Often she raced at one track in the afternoon and at another at night. "The only place that didn't pay us was Aqueduct," Webb says.

A stablehand at the Big A, watching Barbara Jo pose for pictures one afternoon, called her "the travelingest apprentice I ever saw."

But today the rainbow has tarnished, the bubble has

popped. It's all over. Like millions of other American girls, Barbara Jo Rubin sets the alarm five days a week and puts in regular hours at a relatively routine job that could be filled by any girl with a pretty face, a pleasing personality and a basic knowledge of racing. She has a job fit for a woman who has an airlines hostess-geisha mentality, not one who was a pioneer.

Barbara Jo is now an information girl at the Calder Racetrack in Miami. Her duties range from answering questions about track conditions to pointing the way to the rest rooms. The uniform she wears is a parody of her previous fame. She is dressed in a garish orange and lime top that is styled like a racing shirt; to accent that, she wears white hot pants and high white boots.

To those who know her, and who knew her *when*, the Barbara Jo who walks around Calder today is little more than a palpable ghost of the famous girl they remember. Often they refer to her in the past tense, sometimes exaggerating her fame, as one might talk about an idol who has died and passed into legend.

"Two years ago Barbara Jo was the most famous woman in the United States," says Patty Whitmore, a gracious ex-Playboy bunny who shares the duties of the information booth with Barbara Jo.

Sitting in his private box in the grandstands at Calder, Brian Webb, a forty-ish, handsome man in an earthy, hayseed way, sipped a Coke and reminisced about his protégé.

"Can you imagine being the first of anything?" he asks. "Especially a girl being a jockey. . . . She broke the barrier for all female participation in sports. I've seen in the paper today where some girl is playing football out in Nevada."

Naturally, the question of why Barbara Jo stopped racing came up. Is it true, as some of her critics said, that Barbara Jo never really liked racing? That she just became a jockey to catch the eye of a Hollywood producer and, when nobody nibbled, she washed her hands of the dangerous sport?

"She could have been in the movies easily," Webb says. "I could have gotten her a contract. But she didn't want that. She was the most bashful person you ever seen in your life. When the reporters came around for interviews, she'd hide behind a bale of hay. I'd have to go find her and drag her out. The hardest thing I had to do was convince her she had to have publicity. She wanted to be a jockey. She didn't want to be no celebrity."

Webb's opinion may be true, but if Barbara Jo wanted it so badly, then why—when she achieved such a remarkable racing record in such a short time—did she give it all up?

"Her main problem was weight. Barbara Jo, honest to God, would have to be a glutton. I never seen a girl eat so much in my life. She was always a natural lightweight when she was just galloping horses. But then when she started riding, she started to put it on."

Slouching in his chair and propping his legs up against the back of the seat in front of him, Webb chuckles as he recalls the time Barbara Jo was invited to race in Nassau.

"Just before we left for the Bahamas, we went to a Spanish restaurant and she ate a full-course dinner for lunch. Then we got on the plane. Now, we're flying first class, so naturally you get everything from soup to nuts. . . . Well, the last thing I wanted to see was food. She ate her meal and mine on the plane.

"I'd scream at her and cuss her, and it seemed the more I'd do it the worse it would be. It finally got to be funny 'cause you could see the writin' on the wall. She was a young kid then, only nineteen, and she was growin' like a weed. Now look at her. How filled out she is! I kid her about it all the time, sayin', 'Barbara Jo, what've you been doin'?'"

Barbara Jo is five-feet-six and, at that height, it would be difficult for any jockey, male or female, to make his weight. But as she tells it, excess weight is not the reason she quit riding.

To maintain her strength when she was racing, she filled her body daily with B_{12} shots and ten kinds of vitamins. Yet three accidents came in four years. The first occurred in October, 1969, after she had been riding only ten months, when a horse flipped over in the starting gate at Assinaboa Downs in Canada and crushed both her knees. She was ready to return to riding in March of the following year, but at Tropical Park her horse went through the fence—the result was moving blood clots in both legs and another five months on the sidelines.

But it was the third accident that killed any hope she still cherished about resuming her riding career. In the summer of 1971, while riding Junior, her quarter horse, at her farm in Country Club Ranch outside Miami, Barbara Jo was injured when the horse reared up and came down backward. Trapped under the stallion's body, she suffered a broken pelvis.

"Since my pelvis I've had so much pain," Barbara Jo relates. "I get blood clots very easily and my knees aren't very good. Just to ride I have to wrap my legs in bandages." The accident also left her depressed.

Barbara Jo tried her hand at training, but she didn't take to it. So she started to work as a jockey's agent. She discovered rather quickly that she didn't take to this either, that it's tough trying to hustle somebody else's book. "I wouldn't mind asking for myself, but when you have to ask for other people and they don't do well, then it's embarrassing," she confesses.

She tried to stay away from the track, only to learn that there wasn't any other place she wanted to be. "Once you get the dirt in your blood, you can't get it out," she said while distributing programs to the racetrackers who passed her booth. "This way I'm at least useful. I know horses."

Some of Barbara Jo's friends add that the reason she works is that she needs the money. She owns 2½ acres of the seven-acre farm where she lives with her mother, and she wants to hold on to it. What happened to all the gravy she was supposed to have made racing is a touchy subject.

"She done made a fortune and blowed it," is Brian Webb's candid opinion. "Now she's broke. Having to work for a living. After all that money."

Barbara Jo's version is different, of course. "I didn't get as much as people think," she says. "The contract was set up so that Brian would get 20 percent, the agent would get 20 percent, the lawyer would get 10 percent and I'd get the rest. But I didn't make that much because I couldn't stay at a meet and ride the meet and just make money. I had to do too many TV shows and go to testimonial lunches and dinners and stuff like that. So I really didn't get that much." Then she adds, "I did a commercial for Metrecal and got $12,000, but it only ran about a month and a half because cyclamates came out. And they had to take it off the air."

Another reason she didn't get to enjoy her slice of the pie, according to some of Barbara Jo's close associates, was that her father, Robert Rubin, who operates the Miami Sands Motel, managed the bulk of her income and invested it poorly.

He opened a bar called Barbara Jo's Lounge and decorated it with racing colors and pictures of Barbara Jo in the winner's circle. Even the matchbook covers carried her photo. The waitresses wore jockey's silks, and Barbara Jo was supposed to act as hostess. In fact, she spent only one evening there. "I hated it," she said.

Even though Robert Rubin went to flamboyant lengths to publicize the bar—he once hired airplanes and floated banners advertising it—the enterprise was a flop. To Barbara Jo, this represented defeat on her home turf.

Miami has been Barbara Jo's home for all but the first two months of her life. She was born in Highland, Illinois, on November 21, 1949, while her parents were there on a vacation.

Maxine, Barbara Jo's mother, grew up on a farm in Mulberry Grove, Illinois. Her father came from Brooklyn. Because of her last name, Barbara Jo has frequently been described as "a nice Jewish girl," a description that is partially true. Her father is Jewish.

At six Barbara Jo was stricken with polio. She escaped permanent damage but was required to spend six months in a hospital and to wear heavy, leaded shoes throughout grammar school. One can only guess, but it seems at least possible that being forced to face such a frightening illness at such an early age sparked the fiercely independent streak and courage that marked Barbara Jo's career as a jockey.

She displayed a sense of invincibility when only a child. "I never thought anything bad could happen to me," she says, remembering her battle with polio. "I used to say to my mom at the time, 'I don't know why you're prayin'. I'm going to walk. I'm going to walk.'"

To Barbara Jo's delight, part of the therapy recommended by her doctor was that she ride a pony.

When she was eight years old she saw *National Velvet*, which starred Elizabeth Taylor, Mickey Rooney and a horse, and she fell even more in love with horses. "The only person I ever patterned myself after when I was little was Elizabeth Taylor," she admits. "I used to always dream of being her."

That same year, Mr. Rubin, who was then operating a gas station, bought a pony to give rides to the customers' children. They didn't get too many rides; the pony was Barbara Jo's domain.

"She kept trading for bigger and better ponies," her mother recalls. "She was a real sharp trader, and by the time she was fifteen she had traded herself up to a full-size horse."

As a schoolgirl, Barbara Jo's grades were mostly *B*'s and *C*'s. She went to cowboy movies, clipped pictures of horses from magazines and built a collection of show ribbons and awards that overflowed her room and had to be stored in boxes.

"I taught her to sew and she did fairly well," her mother says. "But she made mostly costumes for horses."

Barbara Jo loved playing baseball and football with the boys, racing with them across open fields. Whenever a rodeo came to town, she was always there, eager and ready to join. She was a fairly good calf roper and even rode a few bulls— the little ones, which weigh about 800 pounds—until one gored her in the back. Her mother told her that she had to quit riding bulls or her horse would be taken away.

After graduating from Miami's Coral City High School, Barbara Jo enrolled in a preveterinary course at Broward Junior College. She stayed only one semester. "There was no sense wasting my father's money," she says, "when I wasn't interested. So I quit, and groomed and walked horses at Tropical Park for four hours every morning. Then they'd let me ride them for ten minutes. I didn't get paid either."

The summer following her stint at Tropical Park, she went to tracks in New England as an exercise girl, getting paid three dollars per horse. She averaged seven animals a day. When she returned to Florida, she was given a job exercising horses for Brian Webb.

"She was an exceptional rider," says Webb. "The tough horses would run away from the boys in the morning work-outs. After Barbara Jo got on the tough ones, there were no problems. I think she talks to horses."

Just like many of the other girls who became jockeys, Barbara Jo's interest was aroused when she read about Kathy

Kusner and Penny Ann Early in the newspapers. She decided to take a crack at getting her jockey's license. Rather than lose an excellent exercise girl, Webb put Barbara Jo under contract, and thought nothing more would come of it.

On January 14, 1969, Barbara Jo Rubin made formal application to Ed Pons, the senior steward at Tropical Park. She gave him her three-year contract with Webb, then her birth certificate and then her fee, which was $5.25. The contract was in order, having been signed by her parents because she was only nineteen years old. To qualify as a jockey in Florida, Barbara Jo had to break from the gate and race in the company of other horses for at least an eighth of a mile. This was no problem.

Barbara Jo went to the gate on Webb's Jamie C, a filly that had never started. Jamie C was fractious, yet no one attempted to help Barbara Jo. She controlled the horse. When the gate opened, Barbara Jo sent her to the front and easily outran all her male competitors by a wide margin down the backstretch before pulling up at the quarter pole.

"That girl can really ride," said Pons when he awarded her a temporary license. (She received her permanent license after competing in two bona fide races.)

Two days later Webb had Barbara Jo scheduled to mount a horse named Stoneland, but eleven male jockeys boycotted the race. The boys won the small battle when the race was canceled, but they lost the war when they were each fined $100—with the promise of more and steeper fines if they continued refusing to compete with the girls.

"When she started racing at Tropical Park, I made an

agreement with Saul Silverman, the owner of Tropical, that if she didn't work out, I'd take her off myself and not cause any trouble," says Webb. "Then he got mad 'cause the jocks were on strike and he didn't want me to take her off. He said, 'The hell with them.'"

Tempers flared that week. One jockey tossed a rock through Barbara Jo's dressing room window. The stewards never discovered who did it because the rock was thrown from an enclosed area that the male jockeys used in getting sun.

Webb found himself at the center of a national controversy. "I got letters this high from people all over the country," Webb states, extending his arm to indicate height. "A lot of the women were naturally praising me and the men were knocking me."

It was rumored around Tropical Park that Brian Webb was pushing Barbara Jo because they were lovers. Webb's reputation with the ladies did nothing to quiet these rumors. He has an animal way of looking at a woman or of touching her arm which immediately establishes a sense of intimacy.

Webb denies vehemently that there was anything romantic between Barbara Jo and himself. "It was definitely not a love affair. We had no relationship like that whatsoever."

Trouble began to perk when the jockeys started telling Webb that if he rode Barbara Jo, they wouldn't ride for him. He decided to call their bluff.

"I'm leading trainer practically everywhere I go," Webb says candidly. "One . . . two . . . three, anyway. So I went into the jocks' room and I said, 'I'm going to ask one of you jocks to ride my horse, and if you refuse, you'll never ride a horse for me again.' I said, 'I think you'll have more to lose than I'm going to have to lose.' So I asked George Velasquez, the leading rider. He said, 'Certainly.' He rode my horse."

According to Webb, it was the failures who were against Barbara Jo. The good jockeys didn't give a damn one way or another.

"Barbara Jo has a lot of heart for a girl," Webb explains. "She wasn't scared of anything. After all, when you weigh 110 or 112 and you're on a 1000-pound horse and there's twelve other jocks in there with you, you always think of falling or of somebody running on top of you. That's what worried all the jocks. They thought she might be too weak to handle a horse in a race. They thought she might cause an accident, get somebody killed.

"The jocks' wives were really against her. They thought she would hurt their husbands. Or keep them from making a living, supporting their families, things like that."

Webb took Barbara Jo to the Bahamas next, where one win in two races at Nassau's Hobby Horse Hall track helped settle any question regarding her ability.

She rode her third race—and third winner—at Charles Town, West Virginia, on February 22. "It was the greatest publicity the track ever got," Webb recalls proudly. "You couldn't get a parking place within miles of the racetrack. People walked. She had to have three state troopers escortin' her to the paddock just to keep people away who wanted to grab her clothes as souvenirs. Charles Town racecourse gave her a car in appreciation of what she done for them."

Barbara Jo didn't particularly enjoy the limelight, not the way Mary Bacon does. "The crowds made me nervous," she says. "The people looked at me like I was some sort of kook."

What she remembers most about that race is the way the jockeys tried to test her and how their goading made her even more determined to win. "When I rode there I was a little crazy. Like, I didn't care about going down or anything. And when we went into the turn, they were all looking up at me wondering, 'When is she going to drop out?' They got me hugged in on this turn. I'd just smile at them. And all of a sudden I looked and they'd all dropped back."

Despite her inherent shyness, Barbara Jo's sincere charm and good manners enchant people. Members of the women's liberation movement tried—unsuccessfully—to persuade her to give interviews and speeches and to participate in demonstrations, but she couldn't understand why these women felt restricted in their aspirations.

"If anybody said to me, 'Don't do something,' I'd wait until nobody was looking and then do it," Barbara Jo offers in explanation of why she turned them down.

By the time she hit Aqueduct she had won only seven races—two in Nassau, two at Charles Town, two at Waterford Park and one at Pimlico. Yet she still appeared serene and confident on the morning of March 14.

She dressed alone, in a room assigned to the outriders, and weighed in on a separate scale outside the jockeys' quarters.

Bob Lypsyte, a sportswriter for *The New York Times,* caught the electricity of that day in the story he filed to his paper:

The jockeys, a gantlet of bantam roosters in white pants and T-shirts, smiled at her and introduced themselves. One of them said, "You hit the box yet?" referring to the sweat box.

"Not yet," she said, smiling.

Angel Cordero Jr., swathed in a white terry-cloth robe, his black eyes flashing, asked if she had gloves. It was very cold out on the Aqueduct track. She said she did. "Okay," said Angel solicitously, "now better be careful with those 2-year-old horses, you can never tell what a 2-year-old will do." "Thank you," she said, and weighed in.

It was all very nice but Barbara Jo Rubin needed little help yesterday. Cordero made a great show of tying on her numeral brassard, and the starter, George Cassidy, said loudly, and often, "It's ladies first out of my gate."

As the jockeys entered in the third race reached the saddling area, the nine males suddenly lined up on one side, and chorused, "Ladies before gentlemen."

"Me," said Barbara Jo Rubin. "But I don't know what to do."

And then, of course, she beat them all.

She was riding a bay named Bravy Galaxy in a claiming race for fillies who had never won. Bravy Galaxy, it was said around the track yesterday, had been working out in secret. She was a speedball, she could win with a sack of oats on her back. Buddy Jacobson, the modish, iconoclastic trainer, has often said that a jockey counts for little in a horse race. So, of course, he would be delighted to put Barb up. It would prove his theory, said the misogynists. It will give him publicity, said the smarties. It will keep the big money off Bravy Galaxy, his secret speedball, said the cynics.

And it did. Bravy Galaxy went off at 13–1. Barbara Jo broke her smartly out of the gate, and in the jockey room, in front of the closed-circuit television set, Johnny Rotz took the pipe out of his mouth and Angel Cordero began screaming, "Hey, she look good, she look good."

"Go, go, go," yelled Rotz, pounding his palm, and Cordero, the cheerleader, was now screaming, "All the way, all the way," sometimes in English, sometimes in Spanish, often in both at once.

As Barbara Jo went under the wire a sure winner, the crowd of 25,557 gave a tremendous cheer. It was not until the race was safely won, however, that Barbara Jo showed any emotion. Then spotting Howard (Buddy) Jacobson, she said, "Give me a kiss!" And the blushing Buddy quickly obliged.

The biggest thrill came when the jockeys ambushed her and doused her with a bucket of water, the traditional ceremony after an apprentice rider's first win at the Big A.

Skeptics at Aqueduct were quick to call the triumph a boat race. "Big deal," was the response. "She gets a horse that's pounds the best and manages not to fall off."

While true to form and prediction, Jacobson, who was the leading trainer in 1969, once more told the press that jockeys don't count for much.

"I just wanted to prove a point by bringing Barbara Jo to New York and I think I proved it," Buddy told a reporter. "I've always thought that a jockey represents only 5 percent of the horse's winning races. The horse represents 95 percent. Without taking anything away from Barbara Jo, she had a fast filly under her who was 95 percent of the combination."

But others were willing to concede that the "bug" rider was something exceptional. Writing in the now defunct *Newark Evening News*, Willie Ratner said: "I have seen the greatest jockeys in the country since 1913 and not one has a better style. She 'sits' a horse like Don Meade and that's saying a lot. Her back is absolutely horizontal. Straight as a ruler and she holds her head high. You know what a turtle looks like when it's walking. She also has a pair of shoe strings for reins."

Barbara Jo always maintained that even though she was being put on "live" mounts, the other riders gave her a hard time. "The jocks would say things to me, like, 'I thought it was a guy until I looked over and saw that pigtail.' And I had to take a second look and start ridin' harder."

By April 4, Barbara Jo had chalked up an astonishing eleven victories in twenty-two starts. The owner of Picnic Fair offered her a mount in the Kentucky Derby should the horse make it that far. It didn't. In her total career, Barbara Jo ended up riding in ninety-eight races and winning twenty-eight.

As success usually changes a person, it also changes the way people treat the one upon whom the spotlight shines. Barbara Jo found this to be particularly true with the men in her life.

Prior to her achievements, Barbara Jo had not given much thought to the opposite sex. And, for the most part, the opposite sex responded in kind. Once she beat the boys at Charles Town, though, you would have thought that Mata Hari had invaded thoroughbred racing. The same jockeys who once refused to ride against her, who dismissed her as a little publicity grabber, an aggressive kid who didn't have enough brains to know that girls don't belong on a racetrack, suddenly discovered that Barbara Jo Rubin had sex appeal.

Webb still shakes his head in amazement when he talks

about it. "Before she was famous, I don't think she ever had a date. 'Course all she talked about was horses, and who wants to listen to that all night. But *after*! My God, you never seen so many guys go after her! The jockeys went wild for her. They used to line up outside her dressing room and wait for her to come out."

For the most part, Barbara Jo continued to keep her distance. "I thought most of them were trying to put me on. I thought *wow*! What do they see in me? They must be doin' it cause they think I got bread or something."

Brian Webb was wrong about Barbara Jo's never having had a date. Back when she was an exercise girl in New England, Barbara Jo started seeing a handsome jockey named Willie McKeever. And he surprised everyone—most of all Barbara Jo—by flying from Hot Springs, Arkansas, to Pimlico where she was riding for the express purpose, as he phrased it, "to persuade Barbara Jo to be my wife and give up riding as a profession."

"This nonsense has got to stop," he told reporters when he got off the plane.

Barbara Jo turned him down.

"Billy McKeever's the nicest guy in the world," Barbara Jo says. "Got nothing bad to say against him. I really liked him a lot, but when it came to taking a choice of riding or him, I went whole heart for riding. There were also a few others I had to make a decision about."

Only after she stopped riding did she really learn what it feels like to be rejected rather than being the one who does the rejecting.

After she resettled in Miami, Barbara Jo began dating a boy whom she had known casually at Broward Junior College. The more time they spent together, the more Barbara Jo felt that at last she had met a man who was stronger than she, both physically and psychologically.

"I thought *wow*! I've found something else I can get a high off of. Like, really love besides riding. With him I would wake up in the morning and I'd just smile and feel so good all over.

"He was a weight lifter and wrestling champ and that stuff. But good as gold to me yet. He was the type, like, 'You're my woman. Come here!' "

The strongman went back to school for another term, where he was working toward his degree in physical education. When he returned for summer vacations, things just weren't the same.

"I guess he felt he had competition," Barbara Jo says. "When we were out, people would come up and ask for my autograph. So I figured if things aren't right, I'm not going to stay in a situation and get my head knocked off. I'm going to cut out. So I just said goodbye. I left. I guess it hurts because I don't know what happened. I don't know where I failed. I've been meaning to go over and say, 'Hey, what happened?' So I know it's not me. But I haven't had the nerve yet."

Now Barbara Jo Rubin is floundering. She is far too intelligent and she has seen too much of life to ever be content within the restricted world of the typical American female. At the age of twenty-two, most women are still collecting experiences; in their eagerness for life they dive into new jobs and new love affairs with a verve that's only possible when a person has yet to know a lot of disappointment.

A trainer for a big stable is presently dating Barbara Jo. He is kind and charming, and he is dying to take care of her, but Barbara Jo is a little afraid of all that. Sitting over coffee in the kitchen of her ranch, she talks about it.

"The thing that gets me depressed now is that I'm looking for an easy way out. And I'm not being myself, which is being dependent just on myself. Just on me. I'm trying to find somebody to be dependent on, and I don't like doing that. I sort of feel cheap. It bothers me to think that I have to fall back on that when I can call my own shots."

The next morning she was fumbling among the clutter on the bureau in her bedroom when she picked up a twenty-five-cent Dell horoscope book, one for Scorpios. She explained that in the midst of her depression following the pelvic accident, she bought the book in a drugstore because it was her astrological sign.

Flipping through it, she finds a list of famous Scorpios, and there, in a column that includes Indira Gandhi, Burt Lancaster, Grace Kelly, Pablo Picasso and Katharine Hepburn is Barbara Jo Rubin.

"I was really something, wasn't I?" she says.

4

"I have nothing to hide."

—Jockey Robyn Smith in an interview for *Sports Illustrated*

If you are a celebrity in America today, it is nearly impossible to discard your true life history and replace it with a more colorful, pleasing one. The days of obscurity are gone; parents, relatives, former friends, home towns and even high schools simply won't disappear into filing cabinets as they once did when hired flacks could kill a person's past and create a new one overnight. It was another era when a star like Marilyn Monroe would literally be made from scratch by burying all the facts about her that she did not want known. Things like that can't and don't happen anymore. Because of the swiftness of the media, the past is forever out there somewhere, and it can always be resurrected via the telephone or jet plane.

But Robyn Smith, the most glamorous and well-known jockey in the United States today, still thought she'd try to fudge the facts of her existence. And she has been remarkably successful. Most people don't know that her story about growing up in Hawaii, the daughter of a rich lumberman, and graduating from Stanford before acquiring a contract from M-G-M is nothing more than just a story. The facts as given by Robyn differ greatly from those elicited from others, and her irritation whenever she is asked about them shows clearly. She tries to give the impression that her past isn't important, that she doesn't really care what people say or think. Her guarded reserve falls momentarily when the ghosts and their echoes reappear, but she regains her poise quickly and asserts that, after all, what's most important is that she's a good jockey and she wants mounts.

In an age of plastic people, Robyn Smith is an original, but not authentic. And although her real origin remains obscure, she is very much a personality of the here-and-now. You know when you are in her presence, even if you may wonder exactly *who* the presence is.

In its Babylonian days of puffy press agents and studio hacks, Hollywood itself could scarcely have surpassed the creation of a Robyn Smith. And it is more than coldly ironic that Hollywood as a dream factory has its part in the saga that Robyn created. Above all, she has been the star in her fantasy, as well as the producer, director and impresario. The results please her . . . until the moment in interviews when she is asked about her past. The picture then blurs, and no matter how persistently she is questioned, the answers also become blurred.

Robyn Smith is both a jockey and an actress, and she always plays both roles simultaneously. She is "on" all the time. Her pretty face and seductive smile somehow turn a phrase as cleanly as brass catches light, a fact always obvious when she is interviewed. If she has manufactured illusions —and her family (which she denies is hers) says that she has —they are more than figments to her. They are reality, and it is this reality that Robyn Smith wants back. Because for her it is now the *only* reality.

Robyn has tried to escape her past, but she has succeeded only in abandoning it.

According to reliable data, Robyn Smith was born in San Francisco on August 14, 1942, a date that makes her two years older than she admits. "It was a very painful delivery," says her mother, Mrs. Constance Miller, whose real life has been as eventful as Robyn's fabricated one. "She weighed nine pounds, six ounces. I almost lost my life giving birth to her."

Besides Robyn, there are four other children in the family —a sister, Madalaine Canham, who lives in Los Altos, California; a brother, Fred, who is a naval officer in Jacksonville, Florida; a sister, Sharon, who lives in Salem, Massachusetts; and a brother, Burton, who lives in Hollywood. It was Madalaine who named "Robyn."

"What shall I call her?" Robyn's mother asked, and Madalaine replied, "Call her Melody Dawn." And so that name was recorded. Somewhat embarrassed at having selected such a silly name, Madalaine says today, "I was seventeen at the time. It's a good thing I didn't suggest Melody Lane."

The attending nurses at the hospital where Robyn was born were impressed with the perfect proportions of her small body. "She'll probably be a model," one of them said.

From early infancy Robyn Smith was never to know and enjoy the warmth and comfort of a stable home life. Constance Miller has had four husbands, and even today she is not always precise about the times at which one husband departed and another entered her life.

One of Mrs. Miller's spouses met her one day, proposed the next and then married her the following week. "He had some money," she recalls, "and we moved to Kansas City, where he bought me a ten-room house, and we were society there." The tone somehow connects having money with being society, but it also implies that those were happy times, at least happier than usual—and perhaps steadier.

The fresh whiff of reawakened love did not last long, however, and when Mrs. Miller eventually filed for divorce, she was startled to learn that she had been her husband's sixth wife. "I thought I was number three," she says. "And do you know what? He's up to number ten now. He had a soft spot for the ladies, that one."

Mrs. Miller says today that her health failed after Robyn was born, due in part to the difficulties she had giving birth to such a large baby. Other hardships followed, and the family was temporarily disbanded.

The Oregon Protective Society placed Melody Dawn for adoption with a prosperous Morrow County lumberman and his wife, Mr. and Mrs. Orville L. Smith. This, of course, displeased Mrs. Miller. "They had a shyster lawyer put through these bogus adoption papers," she says bitterly, "and there was money exchanged between the Smiths and the Protective Society. They thought they could buy her soul."

Then, almost as an afterthought, she adds, "A mother

never loved her children any more than I have. Only our Lord knows the agony and ill health dealt out to me."

In 1947, when Robyn was five years old, Mrs. Miller—who was then known as Constance Palm—filed a court action with the Catholic Charities, Incorporated, to have the adoption set aside.

The legal request, which is recorded in *183 Oregon Records 617* of the State of Oregon, was denied by a Morrow County court, but Supreme Court Justice George Rossman later reversed the decision, thereby ordering that Melody be returned to her mother and subsequently placed in a foster home through Catholic Charities. This decision was based on reasoning that a child should be placed for adoption only with a family of the child's religious background. It was a landmark case in Oregon, where it made the front pages of many newspapers.

But what seemed like a victory for Robyn's mother was, in several ways, a defeat, or at least a temporary one. Catholic Charities attempted to keep mother and daughter apart, and there was a period of seven years when Mrs. Miller didn't see her daughter once.

"If anyone ever got a rotten deal, it was this mother," wrote Mrs. Miller in her gusty vernacular to Bill Mulflur, sports editor of the *Oregon Journal*, who had written a story on Robyn's true origins. "These holier-than-thou Catholics go to Mass every morning and then talk about their neighbors all week long. What hypocrisy! A slap in our Lord's face, and that old gal down there at Catholic Charities that took such a dislike to me had never had a child. What the hell would she know about a mother's love? She talked of mothers that would hibernate in bars all day, day in and day out, living with men they weren't married to, and still they would insist they see their children once weekly."

Robyn—or Melody Dawn—was a beautiful child with a particularly winning charm. "She caught the glances," her mother says proudly as she reminisces, recalling that when Robyn was in high school, the students held a contest in which they all brought pictures of themselves that were taken when they were babies, and Robyn won. "They gave her a pair of lacy rubber baby panties as the prize, and she gave them to me."

While a very young child, Robyn developed a case of severe asthma. "She was allergic to cow's milk," says her mother, "and she had to have a special diet. It was terrible when she would have an attack. Even her toenails would get blue."

Two years in succession Robyn was placed in the Doernbacher Hospital in Portland, Oregan, for treatment. She was in grade school then, and because of her illness and frequent absences, she fell a year behind her class. When she graduated from high school in 1961 she was nineteen years old.

The high school years were, in some ways, unsettling for Robyn, for at that crucial period of her life, the years of adolescence when she was becoming a woman, she was again separated from her real family. She lived with five other girls, all foster children, in the home of Frank and Hazel Kucero.

One of Robyn's "foster sisters" remembers those years

fondly. "It was a riot with all the girls," says Louise McNair. She describes Robyn as very popular, with a lot of boyfriends. It is obvious that even then Robyn was somewhat more mature than the others—or at least she thought that she was. "She always went for older men. She went out with college boys when we were living with the Kuceros."

At the Kuceros' Robyn was also known as a tomboy. She was freckled and cute and she loved sports. Softball and volleyball were her favorites. And, like all the other girls who have become jockeys, Robyn loved animals, horses most of all. But because of her persistent trouble with allergies, she couldn't be around them for long. "She'd go out riding one day and she would be sick for a couple of days," recalls Mrs. McNair. The sickness and its frequent spells did not lessen her love for horses, however; if anything, it is likely that it became a hidden, or unknown, persuader in pushing to the fore Robyn's drive to become somebody. As a teenager, that often awkward period when dreams are made and sometimes reluctantly set aside, Robyn knew that she was going to become someone special.

Mrs. Miller and her headstrong daughter saw each other only intermittently during the high school years. Among the mother's personal treasures is a religious card that Robyn sent to her. It was inscribed "To a wonderful mother from one who respects her very much. Lovingly, Melody." On the back she wrote, "Dear Mom, Hope you have a Merry Christmas and a prosperous New Year." Curiously, the word "respects" was written where one might naturally expect to find "love," and even more strange, perhaps, is the wish that the coming year be a "prosperous" one rather than a year of good health, happiness or simply joy. In her then young idea of happiness, Robyn equated money, or prosperity, with happiness and satisfaction, thus linking her to her mother in a way she might not have thought possible.

Robyn also kept in touch with the Orville Smiths while she was in high school. And just before she was about to graduate, they came down from Seattle, where they were living at the time, to give a party for her. "Robyn was nice to her mother," Mrs. Kucero says, "but the Smiths had a little more to offer."

By the time Robyn graduated, her mother had managed to pull things together sufficiently to buy a two-bedroom house in Portland, and she happily made plans to have Robyn come home again. "I bought her a beautiful wristwatch for graduation," her mother relates somewhat bitterly, remembering that it hadn't occurred to her then that Melody would not want to return home. Their hopes—or at least Mrs. Miller's—of being a real family again were broken, for in the meantime Robyn had already made plans to move to Seattle to live with the Smiths. "Behind our backs she called the Smiths because she knew they had money," Mrs. Miller says. "I didn't know a thing about it until a friend told me."

When Mrs. Miller did inquire about her plans, Robyn's reply was acidic and succinct: "Go to hell, Mom!"

Louise McNair remembers that this two-sidedness was a prominent trait in Robyn's personality at the time. "She played both ends against the middle." Robyn thus took full advantage of her own wounded feelings at having been placed in a foster home. While her plan to live again with the Smiths might seem devious to some, particularly in light of her not telling her mother, the idea apparently seemed perfectly logical to Robyn. She had long known that she wanted something better, something more secure, than what life had given her thus far, and she was intelligent enough to know that she would find a way to get it.

She knew, too, how to get other things that she wanted. Robyn asked Mrs. Miller for twenty dollars to buy graduation pictures. Her mother's opinion at getting the short end of the bargain is obvious when she tells what happened. "She gave a wallet-size picture to me and a big one to the Smiths—with *my* money!"

Against her mother's wishes, but in accordance with her own, Robyn did move to Seattle to live with the Smiths. They rejoiced at the reunion, and their happiness was expressed in a vacation they all took to Hawaii. For a time, at least, Robyn was part of a family. The happiness was short-lived. Once when Louise McNair was visiting in Seattle, she tried to locate Robyn and learned that she was no longer living with the Smiths. She had moved to an all-girls' residence. Why she did this is not exactly clear.

While living in Seattle, Robyn returned to Portland to visit the Kuceros. By that time she had already changed her name at least once; she was then known as Caroline Smith. The Kucero clan took Robyn out to dinner, having been instructed by her prior to their leaving that they were to call her by her new name. "Now, don't you dare call me Melody," she directed. "My name is Caroline now."

Mrs. Kucero's brother-in-law teased Melody-Caroline-Robyn throughout dinner. "No matter what," he said, "you'll always be Melody to us."

Knowing Robyn well, the Kuceros sensed—correctly, it seems—that she had had some kind of falling out with the Smiths. And they knew, too, that she didn't want to talk about it.

"After she left home, I saw her once on the street," Fred Miller, Robyn's brother, says. "I spoke to her, but she didn't answer me." Despite this rejection, he and his sisters seem sympathetic in their understanding of Robyn's burning desire to structure a new, more pleasant life for herself. Such an act involves forgetting the past, of course, and Robyn has tried to do just that. The family understands her desire, but it seems natural, as well as logical, that they cannot help feeling she is wrong. "Even though we are essentially strangers, I feel a certain loyalty to her," Fred says.

Madalaine feels the same way, although she hasn't seen her since Robyn was eight years old. When Robyn was racing at Santa Anita, Madalaine wanted to talk to her, but she was fearful that Robyn might think she was trying to blow her cover. "She's painted this beautiful picture of herself," Madalaine acknowledges, "and I wouldn't want to spoil it." It is obvious that as a sister she wants to reach out and touch, but Robyn simply doesn't want to feel. "We're not a close family," Madalaine adds. "Mother didn't see her brother for thirty-five years. They were brought together by the efforts of the Red Cross when he was dying."

Louise McNair, who now lives in Connecticut, would like

to get in touch with Robyn, but she is hesitant. "I'd call her Robyn, of course," she says. "I think if I talked to her by name it would start a war."

If Melody Dawn and Caroline Smith are relative unknowns, Robyn Smith is the opposite. Without doubt she is the best-known woman jockey, and men *and* women follow her career closely. Robyn was on the cover of *Sports Illustrated* last year, and the lengthy article about her was later condensed in *Reader's Digest*. She has been interviewed by sportswriters and feature writers throughout the country; wherever she races, she is news. Because she is unique, pretty (a fact mentioned in all the articles), and *good*, she is considered hot copy. Wherever she appears, whether she wins or not, a Robyn Smith article is a sure thing for the sports pages.

And yet, no matter how many thousands of words are written about her, there is an uncomfortable inkling that something vital, something integral, is missing. There is a feeling that Robyn is holding back—that she is telling the reporter only what she wants him to know, and thus print, and no more.

For Robyn's fans, the mystery of who she really is remains. The more she is interviewed, the less she seems to make clear. And this serves only to deepen the mystery. Her answers are pat because the questions are usually pat. Once in a while she trips up on the facts and sometimes she gives conflicting answers, but most of the time she knows exactly what she is going to say.

The Robyn Smith story as told by those who say they are

her family is different in every way from the one that the top woman jockey tells the world. In the *Sports Illustrated* article, Frank Deford, the author, stated, "By her spare account, her parents both died of natural causes a couple of years ago." In a second piece, Pat Rogerson's "More About Robyn," which appeared in *The Racing Form*, Robyn said, "I was born in San Francisco and my parents died when I was quite young." Robyn herself was in all probability responsible for the several discrepancies in the stories of these two men. Deford wrote that the bit about her being a former starlet was just "poppycock." Robyn told Rogerson: "You've heard me referred to rather glowingly as a 'former starlet.' Not really. Oh, I was interested in acting and was actually signed by M-G-M, but all I did was go to acting school. I never made a film. The reason I didn't continue with film work is simple. It bored me."

The truth is that although Robyn might at one time have had ambitions to become an actress, she was never a starlet and was certainly never signed by M-G-M. She was a member of the acting workshop at Columbia Pictures and she did know Martin Ransohoff, the head of Filmways, a major production company. He was not her agent, as she has stated, but he clearly thought she had a good future in films. "I believe if she had stayed in Hollywood big things could have happened for her."

Big things did happen for Robyn.

At the Big A, regarded in racing circles as the top track in America, she was the leading United States jockey in 1972. The six who topped her were all men and, as Deford noted in *Sports Illustrated*, they were all foreigners.

Speculation aside, there are at least three factors about Robyn that are uncontestably true: (1) she has an understanding and a "feeling" about horses; (2) she possesses a great talent for riding, and (3) she is a strikingly attractive woman. You don't have to look twice to be convinced that she probably could have had a career in the movies if she had wanted it badly enough.

She is five-foot-seven, much taller than the other jockeys, male or female. She has the poise and carriage of a fashion model. And like many models, she has no breasts. Her brown hair shines and highlights the green eyes that in turn accent her dimples and freckles. When riding, her weight varies between 105 and 108 pounds, but she does not really appear skinny—merely thin, as tall women often do. It seems likely that her natural weight should be in the area of 125 to 130 pounds, so it is particularly obvious to others, especially jockeys, that Robyn goes to great lengths to keep her weight down.

Her regimen of daily exercise and diet is not too different, if at all, from that of other women who want to stay thin. Robyn eats cottage cheese, grapefruit, lean ground beef that is broiled, eggs, ice cream; once in a while she has coffee. She claims that she can eat anything she likes and still keep her weight at 111, and that when she goes off her diet—which is not often—she never gains more than three pounds. "I'm a rare physical individual, and I'm not really trying to be narcissistic about it. It's just that I'm very unusual in that way."

Where Robyn Smith is not unusual, where she is like most jockeys, is in her mental reserve, her ability to devote all her attention to her profession. Except for brandy and an occasional glass of wine, she does not drink. Jockeys are known to go to great, even dangerous extremes to keep their weight down. Many consume laxatives the way other people devour Hershey bars. Pills are another way of shedding pounds. According to writer Frank Deford, "Robyn's system is littered with the residual effects of weight pills, water pills, hormone pills, big pills, little pills, pill pills that she gobbles indiscriminately."

Robyn Smith has said that she has always had an interest in horses, but had no ambition to become a jockey until 1969. While she was in acting school—according to her version—she dated a young man who had a horse with Bruce Headley, a trainer at Santa Anita. "I came out to watch it work one morning," she says, "and I saw a girl galloping a horse and couldn't believe my eyes. It never dawned on me women could be a part of racing. I've always had a tremendous affinity for animals of all kinds, and I really got excited about the possibility of working at the racetracks." She asked Bruce Headley if he needed an exercise girl, but he didn't at the time. "I think I told him I'd been riding for years, which I hadn't," she was to tell Pat Rogerson.

About a year later Headley gave Robyn a job galloping horses. Robyn admits that she was learning as much from the horses as they were learning from her. "Thank God it was dark those mornings and nobody really saw what I looked like on a horse. After I'd been working for Bruce for about four months, he got his first good look at me galloping a colt one morning. 'You don't know too much about working a horse, do you?' he said. I admitted I didn't, but he stuck with me and I gradually learned what I was doing."

Robyn became serious in her attempt to become a jockey when the Kathy Kusner hullabaloo became headlines. Her interest in an acting career vanished, and she was determined then to become not simply a jockey, but the best. She played hookey from acting school, she said, to work at the track, and she drove fifty miles to get there to her job that was without pay.

Her first mount came in 1969, when Kjell Qvale called and asked if she wanted to ride at Golden Gate. Robyn jumped at the chance. She received her license that year at Golden Gate, where she had her first mount and finished second.

The California fair circuit kept Robyn busy for a while after she left Golden Gate. In that breakthrough year she was a novelty and an impetus for increased attendance, as all the girl jockeys were. But after several two-week stands on the fair route, Robyn was already anxious to make the big time. "I decided that if I was going to make it in racing, it was going to be first cabin or not at all," she told Rogerson. So she packed and headed for New York.

She had grit and guts and determination then, as she has now, but Robyn admits she was afraid when she first arrived at Belmont. "Talk about a greenie. I remember getting out of the cab in front of Belmont Park and being terrified. 'What in the world am I going to do here?' I thought. But after about a week I got a job galloping horses, and then I got a tremendous break when trainer Allen Jerkens put me on some of his horses." Again, to Rogerson.

This proved to be a turning point in her career. Allen Jerkens is a highly regarded trainer, and when he put Robyn on horses, others began to notice her. "The fact that he put her on live horses," says Frank Wright, another respected trainer from Tennessee who knew Robyn when she was just starting out and who remains one of her best friends and staunchest boosters, "was like the Good Housekeeping seal."

Although Jerkens still regards Robyn as a weak finisher, in spite of all her successful races, he was quick to recognize that she has a way with horses. She rated her mounts well and was always strong out of the gate. "She gives a horse a chance," he says. The weak-finisher criticism is one that Robyn shares with all the other women jockeys. Most of them simply don't have the great muscular strength that is needed in the stretch, so, like Robyn, they have to work to develop other talents. "Most women can't do it right," Robyn admits in talking about women on horses. "The trouble is that the women who generally would be best at riding are the big heavy broads who could never make the weight."

With a casualness that suggests it was simply the next link in a natural chain of events, Robyn has said that her working for Allen Jerkens led to her "association with Alfred Vanderbilt." This "association," as she calls it, gave her career a vital boost.

Vanderbilt, who is sixty years old and still quite attractive, is chairman of the prestigious New York Racing Association. He openly professes his admiration for Robyn as a jockey. "I wanted to see her make it," he says. "She deserves to make it. She's just plain good, and she cares." He admired her even before she rode for him as his regular rider for several months last year. There was then a short break in their relationship, but she has ridden for him since; one of her wins for Vanderbilt was in a stakes race at Santa Anita. His praise of her talent is generous. He knows that she will continue to make it—and make it "big." "Her life is very full," he once remarked to *Sports Illustrated*'s Deford, recognizing the steely determination that is one of her trademarks. "She knows just what she wants to do, and she's going to do it. I asked her once what she wanted most, and she said she wanted to be the best rider in the world."

Then, as an afterthought that is also characteristic of Robyn's conversation, he adds, "Best in the world, just like that. I suppose she would have said the best rider in the world *ever*, but she just didn't think of that at the moment."

As for being the best jockey *ever*, there have been moments when Robyn surely has considered that. She told a reporter that she really isn't impressed by anything, that in her own way she is an iconoclast ("I guess I'm the biggest iconoclast I know"). But Robyn, in truth, is quite impressed with herself. Considering her talents, there is nothing remarkable about this. She would have to be impressed with herself or she could never have come as far as she has. And it isn't conceit, either, for Robyn does not entertain a Mark Spitz look-at-me complex. She simply knows that she is good, yet doesn't let it go at that. She is always trying to improve.

There are others besides Jerkens, Wright and Vanderbilt who are impressed with Robyn Smith the jockey. Angel Cordero, one of the consistently top riders at the Big A, said that

Robyn had improved 80 percent in only a year, a remarkable feat for any athlete. "Robyn rides good," he says. "She can rate a horse and push [hand ride], and she can switch the stick." Deford noted that Robyn could not switch the whip from one hand to the other without first placing it in her mouth (a common procedure among inexperienced jockeys until they have mastered the passing technique), but this was intended merely to describe the way Robyn rides. Her technique has improved and is getting better all the time.

Such improvement would most likely come from experience, but Robyn tends to discount that. "Experience is important only in the early stages of a rider's career, to give him or her confidence," she says. "Later it has little to do with one's success. The proof is that so many jockeys keep riding for years without improving. I felt from the start that I had it. I have the talent. Last year I got experience riding races. But I don't think I'm much better this year because of it. What I gained was confidence."

Something that does have a bearing on a rider's success, she thinks, is an affinity for horses. According to Robyn, this theory hasn't an iota more weight with women than with men. "Rapport with horses isn't a matter of sex, but of the individual," she said in an early interview—when the press got to her more easily than it does now. "I feel that I have this rapport, but not because I'm a girl. I think horses run kindly for me, although I couldn't tell you why. Maybe it's my touch. And sometimes, when I breeze a horse, I feel almost telepathic communication with him. I just have to think 'more speed,' it seems, and the horse will turn it on. It could be something I do unconsciously with my hands that triggers him."

Robyn is, of course, very fond of horses, more fond of them perhaps than she is of people. In part, this has led to her reputation as a loner. In Terence Rattigan's *Separate Tables*, there is a tweedy, stocky, sensible-shoes woman who admits that she has always liked horses because people sort of frighten her; that she is afraid when she is around humans, but isn't that way with animals. Robyn's social life, such as it is, centers on the track; away from the track her socializing seems minimal.

When she is racing at Aqueduct, Robyn lives in an apartment in Floral Park, Long Island, about twenty minutes from the Big A. She has three pet rats, Peanuts, Pepper and Paprika, that travel with her (she carries them in a handbag). She plays an occasional game of golf—in the low 90's—sometimes with her valet. She is reputedly a good surfer and an excellent swimmer, and she is also known as something of a pool shark. Robyn won an important amateur pool tournament—from men—in California. The prize was an expensive cue. "The sad part about that," she says, "is that the cue was stolen from me. Even worse, it was in my car, and that was stolen too."

Horses instead of men seem to occupy Robyn's spare time. Grazing them is her hobby, "because, you know, I like them. I like to graze the horses I ride, especially the ones that win for me. . . . I like to be around the animal that won for me because that means a lot to me." Knowing that an outsider might consider this a strange hangup, Robyn adds, "I'm not so hung up on it that I'm sick. When I do it, I just do it because that is what I feel like doing," she told writer Deford.

"I just like to be alone. I don't think I'll ever get married. I'm just a loner. I've had friends who see me grazing, and they come over and want to talk with me. It doesn't occur to them that I might just want to be alone with a horse."

Robyn Smith has all the attributes and assets of the top male jockeys, except she is taller than most of them. Her forte is her sharp ability to rate a horse. Jockeys who know how to rate equines can tell just how fast the horse is running. This skill is vital to a jock's success because many horses are stronger finishers than starters. Therefore, if a horse breaks too fast a jockey must be aware of it and restrain the animal. This talent renders Robyn particularly valuable in the morning, when she has been known to work as many as ten horses and averages six or seven, including some stakes horses. If a trainer tells her to work a horse in a mile at 1:42, she will usually hit it right on the nose; when she doesn't, she is rarely off by more than one-fifth of a second. "Amongst all the girls that are riding, there ain't too many that can compare with her," says Tony Delvecchio, her agent. "She knows a little somethin' about a horse. She can tell you something about a horse. A lot of girls can't. She can get a quick feel of a horse and tell you if the horse needs blinkers."

Robyn admits this is true, just as she freely acknowledges that some jockeys don't "have it." Her ability to size up a mount, to know how the horse is feeling and how it will react, is recognized by all who know her. "I can walk into the barn and sense when a horse has something bothering him."

She can tell "by the look in his eyes. And I'm usually right, even though he may look fine to his handlers. In a race I can sometimes almost will a horse to do his best without doing anything physical. I also find that riding in races is a great way to get rid of hostility."

Any hostility that Robyn Smith harbors is directed in one of several ways: at the foolish prejudices that keep her from getting more mounts because of her sex; toward the snoopy people (the interviewers and sportswriters who pry into her past); and, perversely, away from her family, whom she consistently denies by simply not acknowledging them.

There are jokes about Robyn just as there are about almost any celebrity. But none seems to faze her. Publicity is part of her life now, although she does little to feed the publicity mills—little, that is, except ride and win. She doesn't want publicity, Robyn says adamantly. What she wants are more mounts! Her avoidance of the press and of people in general has won for her a number of disparaging labels. Like it or not, and deserved or not, Robyn Smith is popularly known as The Bitch.

The Bitch, obviously, has several connotations, although the label is not so uncomplimentary if you think of Henry James or Paddy Chayefsky's use of it to refer to the goddess Success. It cannot be denied that Robyn Smith is a success and that she regards herself as such, even though she says, "I'm going to be highly successful, so there'll be a much more interesting life for them to write about ten years from now." Perhaps she hopes this will stop reporters from writing about her past and her present; in a way, it is a nearly perfect escapism. But reporters are going to write about her now, anyway, and Robyn knows it. She will probably continue to tell just what she wants to tell and invent where she believes the truth is not good enough. She has literally invented herself, and no one is going to change the plan, let alone the creation.

Any Queen Bee complex that Robyn might have is justifiably deserved. She knows in her own mind who and what she is, just as she knows what others think of her. Once a writer, attempting to persuade her that she should permit him to ghost her autobiography, was put off when Robyn asked him why he didn't write about one of the other women jockeys—Arline Ditmore or Donna Hillman, for example. "Donna Hillman? The pretty one?" he asked. "No, I'm the pretty one," Robyn replied.

Pretty, yes—and successful, talented, dedicated, a newsmaker and newsworthy . . . all these are Robyn Smith. She goes her way and the world goes its way, and out in San Francisco her mother waits patiently for her daughter to call.

5

*Patty Barton, to a reporter: "Thoroughbred horses are
like women. With some of them, if you demand something
of them you might as well move the Rock of Gibraltar. But
if you ask something of them, they'll move that rock!"*

Please don't call me a jockette," Patty Barton said as she
fished a child's faded blue polo shirt and a pair of muddy
socks from behind the couch in the living room of her clut-
tered trailer. "Jockette reminds me of kitchenette or something like that. It sounds like you're just a part of something.
Like there's something left to be desired."

Patty bristles at any slight suggestion that she might be
just a sideshow attraction in the male-dominated world of
racing. She'll stack her riding credentials any day against
those little guys down at the track. After all, two seasons flying off broncs and bulls in rodeos, followed by a year of
belting home God-forsaken cripples in the bushes, not to
mention four years hustling mounts on pari-mutuel tracks,
plus a total of five years of getting up every morning at five-
thirty to gallop horses—well, it's not exactly *My Friend
Flicka.*

The rigors of a tough, outdoor life show strongly in her taut, muscular five-foot-two frame and in her skin, heavily freckled and raw from years and years in the sun. One's first impression is that she scrubs with a Brillo pad. Patty's rich brown hair is cut short, casually. She doesn't bother to set it because it would only get mussed up by her riding helmet. But for special occasions—such as one of her divorce hearings —she fluffs it out with a hairpiece or tucks it under a wig. Then she accents her beautiful blue eyes with a touch of shadow and a few lingering flicks of mascara.

To Patty, the "sport of kings" never held the glowing promise of fame and glamour that it has to many other women jockeys. Racing is just a job to her, but one that she genuinely likes and at which she excels. Most importantly, it pays well, and that means a lot when one has three children to feed and clothe and educate.

"I'm a realist," she says. "I find no joy in laying up on the side of a hill looking at the clouds. So in this way I have no imagination, no fantasy life whatsoever. My dreams are not daydreams or pipe dreams. They are things that are possible. I've always had everything I ever wanted because I never wanted very much. Like the trailer I live in right now. I bought exactly the trailer I wanted. The cheapest two-bedroom trailer I could find. And then I redid it."

Few people would be happy to call Waterford Park, West Virginia, their home. But Patty is. She races there all year round.

Her blue and white economy-size trailer is lined up in a dismal row with others of its type on a bleak hillside that overlooks the racecourse. Those who live in the development

—racetrackers, primarily—seem somehow oblivious to the heavy gray smoke and the nauseous smell of sulfur dioxide floating across the Ohio River from the several steel mills that skirt the nearby town of East Liverpool, a community that surpasses its namesake in England for unrelieved ugliness.

Inside the trailer Patty calmly tried to bring order from chaos as she picked up tennis shoes, jeans, coloring books and whatever else was in her path. She was assisted by her three children, Leah Ann, Donna, and Jerry, the youngest. "I don't have the neatest house," Patty says without any hint of apology. "I never will. But having a neat, clean house is not important to me. Having a livable house is."

Patty Barton knows that Waterford Park is little more than a dump. It is also one of the few places that have racing throughout the year. So she figured, correctly, that if she established herself there, she wouldn't always have to be hustling the way most of the jockeys do.

"I'm a big fish in a little pond," Patty says. "I'm an important person around here. I ride live stock. And I make a decent living. Last year I made $25,000. 'Course that's before my agent, valet, jocks guild and taxes. I took home about half of that."

Sitting down at her formica-topped kitchen table, Patty pulled out her wallet and started to deal out her credit cards —two for gas, one Master Charge and one from United Airlines. "I don't use them very often. But to me they represent security. At least they trust me."

After several years of leading a ramshackle existence, not really knowing where the next cent was coming from (for a while things were so bad that Patty had to place her children with friends), she gloats in the possession of such middle-class items as credit cards. To her they represent more than credit.

Her price for such security is working at Waterford Park, a hugely impersonal racetrack forty miles from Pittsburgh. The track squats in the Allegheny Mountains where Pennsylvania, Ohio and Virginia merge.

"It's like working at a factory," Patty says. "You check in at a certain hour and you see the same people doing the same thing every day. I get sick and tired of galloping horses. I get sick and tired of coming to the jocks' room. But when I get tired of galloping horses in the morning and I still have a few more to go, I tell myself, 'Barton, you used to pay two dollars an hour to ride a horse. So you shut up and enjoy it. You're doing it for free now.'"

Patty arrived at Waterford Park 2½ years ago, having flown to Pittsburgh from the West. "I'll never forget the stares I got at the Pittsburgh airport when I got off the plane in my cowboy suit with my Stetson hat and boots and all," Patty laughs.

She left her beige sixteen-foot trailer with one friend in California and her '61 Cadillac with another. The only other possessions she had, and which she brought with her, were a pack trunk, a bird cage with her dog in it and a three-by-five locker covered in fake yellow and black leopard. The locker is now stained and peeling with age, but Patty keeps it prominently displayed under the window in her living room because it reminds her of how far she's come.

Patty soon noticed that many of the employees at Waterford Park, the "backstretchers," look alike, with cauliflower ears and no chins. They also seemed mentally slow, even for stable help. When she asked about this, she was told that many of the help are hillbillies who come down from the West Virginia mountains. "I was told they go in for a lot of incest up there in the hills," she said.

She wasn't at Waterford very long before she realized that she was going to have to fight for her place among the clique of jockeys at the track.

When she arrived at Waterford Park she was twenty-six, older than most of the jocks against whom she was competing. On top of that, she was much more serious than the girl jockeys they had encountered and, worse still, she was good.

"There's a direct relationship to how well a jock is doing in the standings to how well I get along with him. If he's ahead of me, I get along with him okay. If he's under me, he doesn't like me very well."

In various little ways the jocks let her know that they didn't like the idea of women messing with their sport. They'd bump into her or drop in front of her or yell "Bitch!" as she was coming down the stretch.

So Patty decided early that if she didn't let them know how tough she was, she'd be fair game for whatever kind of abuse they wanted to heap on her.

One night a jockey named Clifford Thompson started bothering Patty, knocking into her along the backstretch and finally cracking her across the rear end at the quarter pole. Patty rode the race out and then laid wait for him on the track. But Thompson outfoxed her by pulling up further down the stretch and slipping quickly into the building.

"I'm fixin' to slap me a jock," Patty told the clerk of scales as she ran off the track.

"There ain't nothin' I can do about it," he said.

Patty ducked into the male jockeys' room. When Clifford came through the door, she nailed him. The fight was on.

"We were punching and kicking and grabbing each other," Patty said. "I got a bloody nose. There were masses of blood on the wall, splotches the size of a silver dollar on the floor. We didn't stop until somebody got ahold of him and somebody got ahold of me."

Shortly after the fight was broken up, one of the stewards walked in and demanded to know what had caused the fracas. Patty calmly pulled down her underpants and showed him the welt on her right cheek caused by Thompson's whip.

The next day the stewards fined Clifford fifty dollars and Patty twenty-five. Clifford was penalized twice as much because he struck Patty with a piece of equipment on the track during a race.

"He absolutely blew his cool over getting fined twice as much as I did, especially since the fines are published in *The Racing Form* so everybody knew," Patty gloated. The management did tell Patty, though, that if such an incident ever occurred again, she was to call the track nurse to examine her instead of dropping her drawers in front of the stewards.

"You know, a lot of the guys say there's no way they can win fightin' me," Patty commented. "Because if they did whip me, what in the hell did they do? They whipped a girl. So they are a woman beater. But the way I feel about it, once I'm in that jocks' room, it isn't sexes. It's not like I am stupid enough being a woman to fight a man. I don't think of it that way at all. We each weigh in the neighborhood of 110, so it's pretty equal."

There is a marked difference, Patty feels, between men and women as far as strength is concerned, but because of her unusual physique, she doesn't categorize herself with the rest of the feminine gender. "I'm exceptional in that I have a build instead of a figure," she said, looking down at her broad, muscular chest and her narrowly-set pelvis. "As you can see, I have no rear end. If I buy women's pants, they are size three."

There seems to be something in Patty's genes that sets her apart from most other women. From childhood on she has thought, acted and felt differently from other girls. Since she is adopted and has never met her real parents, she has no way of knowing why she is as she is. Yet she does know that she has a high IQ, and she knows, too, that she has a strong sense of independence and a hell-bent enthusiasm for such masculine interests as baseball, football and, of course, horse-racing.

There is no trace of bitterness toward the mother who abandoned her. Patty Barton is so proud of the human being that she has created out of so little opportunity that she doesn't brood about something over which she had no control. "Out there somewhere my real mother is wondering what happened to me, wondering what sort of person I became. But I know who I am."

According to Patty, when Frank and Lillian Slattery

brought home a two-month-old baby girl from the New York Foundling Home to their modest residence in Belmore, Long Island, they planned on raising a soft, feminine, Shirley Temple kind of girl. The Slatterys are decent people cut from simple blue-collar cloth. They are guarded and somewhat conservative, and their world does not extend far beyond the boundaries of the family.

When Patty was eight her parents moved to Miami, where her father now works for the Superior Window Company, building Jalousies, windows made of slats of glass that roll out instead of moving up and down. Her mother is a sweet, shy person who was well into middle-age before she ever wrote or cashed a check—and did it then only with Patty's encouragement and guidance.

Patty's parents took her to a rodeo when she was eight. One look at all that color and excitement and the spectacle of the prancing, graceful horses, topped by the diving and the running and the roping, and Patty was hooked. "I was just one of those kids who loved horses. I drew pictures of them, read books about them and all my speeches in class were associated with horses. I collected pop bottles a jillion times to save toward a horse. I hung out any place I could find a horse. At fourteen I got a job working for a veterinarian for large animals and saved every cent. When I was fifteen I bought my first horse. I paid $80 and sold him six weeks later for $150 in order to buy a better horse." She owned four horses in all while she was growing up.

"One thing I think should be encouraging to any young girl with the desire to get into the horse racing field," she added, "is the fact that I myself didn't come from any special horsey background. I was born in the city. Always raised in town. Didn't live close to a racetrack. My folks disliked horses, and I had no help from them whatsoever. So any girl even living in New York City who wanted to make horses her life could do it because I am living proof that it's possible."

When Patty wasn't hanging around horses she was usually out playing with the boys. "I've been riding for quite some time," she said, "and I can honestly say I've had more injuries from playing baseball than I had from fooling around with horses. This here is from baseball," she said, pointing to a lump on her forehead. "The broken teeth are from football. The broken toe is from baseball, and I've had numerous sprains at other times."

During her senior year in high school Patty also worked as a telephone operator while keeping her job with the vet. All this work did not interfere with her scholastic standing, however, for she was graduated in the top 10 percent of her class. As soon as she got out of school she made plans to join the IXL Ranch Show, and the day before she went away, she told her father that she was leaving. "He became very upset and said I couldn't go because he said that he was responsible for me until I was twenty-one. It was then he told me that I was adopted. I kind of suspected it all along because my birth certificate didn't look like other people's. You could tell from the ink that the name had been filled in later than the date."

As earnestly as he tried, Patty's father couldn't dissuade her. Finally she told him, "When you get back from work tomorrow, I'm not going to be here." And the next day she left.

Patty loved the freedom the rodeo gave her. She traveled throughout the northern and midwestern states, mostly saddle bronc riding, and then driving a truck to make ends meet. Often called "the suicide circuit" because of the incredibly high number of men who are maimed or killed in the arena, rodeos are unlikely places for women. They are also big business. In America there are approximately 600 professional outfits that cover the nation; in addition to rodeo schools, there are nearly 100 colleges that belong to the National Intercollegiate Rodeo Association. These offer courses in such diverse and chilling activities as wild horse racing, chuck wagon racing, bareback and saddle riding, steer wrestling, calf roping and barrel racing, none of which is thought to be requisite in the Ivy league.

Barrel racing is a woman's specialty. The girls ride one at a time around a triangular course marked with three barrels, usually large oil drums, which are set about 100 feet apart. The rider must completely circle each of the barrels, and the winner is the one who does it in the quickest time.

Patty Barton liked the rodeo and remembers it with fondness. "It was good at the time. I saw adventure. I met people. But I'd never trade the track for the rodeo."

The following November, when Patty was eighteen, she married Charlie Barton, a saddle bronc rider and a cowboy. Leah Ann, their first child, was born on August 23, 1963, the same month that Patty and Charlie began jobs as grooms in Los Angeles. "I've compared the job of being a groom many times to being a nurse," she says. "You do everything in your power to make that animal in your charge happy. You notice all the details about him. For instance, you notice one day his bowel movements change. So you know that a change has taken place in that horse. A woman is more conscious of these things. A man—he'll go in and get the job done and get out of there. To a woman, that's *her* horse."

Patty played another season of trick riding in the western states and then had two more children. Donna was born on April 12, 1966; Jerry came a year later, on April 15, 1967.

The next year Charlie ran off with Patty's "best friend." So Patty filed for divorce. Today she looks at her ability to judge men with a note of ironic humor: "Line twelve men up in a row and I'll pick the bastard."

In May, 1968, Patty went to Ruidose, New Mexico, where she groomed horses in the morning and then worked as a cocktail waitress at night. Five months later she put her truck-driving experience to work again, hauling feed to the track. And in that month she also got an exercise boy's license and galloped horses.

After all her experience from the rodeo days, Patty thought that galloping horses would be a snap, but she soon learned that it's a tough job. "I don't know how many times I quit," she smiled. "If they didn't try buckin', then they'd try runnin' off. Or they'd try to drop you comin' back."

Patty applied for her jockey's license in February, 1969, and received it in April. "I was gettin' a dollar a head galloping horses and they paid fourteen dollars for riding a race, so that fourteen dollars in my first paycheck meant fourteen horses I didn't have to gallop."

Included in Patty's first riding contract was a clause that

stated: ". . . said minor [Patty was twenty-four at the time] agrees not to leave the said service of his employer during the said term of service and to faithfully, honestly, and industriously serve." When Patty was standing in the steward's office signing her contract, an old racetracker leaned over her shoulder and said, "You know, signing this contract is a whole lot like getting married."

"Yeah," countered Patty, "but one thing also about this contract is that I can lease it out for thirty days for a meet." She had been very careful to work out an arrangement with her contract holder that enabled her to go somewhere else with lease papers supplied by him.

As the first woman jockey in New Mexico, Patty got a lot of attention, but no mounts that amounted to anything. Even more so than in the East, trainers and owners were reluctant to hire her, a *female*. So Patty started to look around for a place where she could show her talents as a rider.

"Pikes Peak was the worst meet I knew of," Patty said later. "They had low purses—like $500—and night races five times a week. Besides that, it was very near still winter, so there was a lot of racing that was both cheap and under bad conditions. I knew that meant there would be fewer jockeys, and the ones that would be riding wouldn't be the best. So I knew I'd have a better chance."

On the way to Colorado, Patty's car broke down just outside of Caradoso. She sold it at a gas station for thirty dollars. Since she couldn't carry all her possessions, she gave part of her belongings to a woman who was headed back to Sundland Park. The woman agreed to drop them off with some of Patty's friends.

Then Patty plunked down twenty dollars for a bus ticket to Pueblo, Colorado, the off-track to Pikes Peak. Racetracks often use another nearby course that is not running races at the time to stable horses they cannot accommodate. There is usually more of a chance to gallop horses in the morning because most jocks gravitate toward the main track.

Two days after her arrival in Pueblo, Patty was working a quarter horse filly out of the gate when the horse slipped over backward and landed on her ankle. The accident put Patty on crutches for the next week. During this period, since she had less than $100 in reserve, she slept in tack rooms to save on living quarters.

As soon as she was well and fit again, Patty applied for her jockey's license, only to discover that many stewards were highly suspicious of the morals of any girl thought tough enough to be a jockey. "They asked me if my contract holder was married or divorced," she said. "I told them I didn't think that information was pertinent to the application."

"Well," said one of the stewards, "we'll think about your application."

In the meantime there was a fair at Cheyenne Wells in Colorado, so Patty went there and lied to the stewards, claiming that she did have a license.

She rode nine races at Cheyenne Wells, and she won three and placed third twice. The stewards at Pikes Peak were sufficiently impressed so that, upon her return, Patty was awarded a license on the spot.

Nobody gave her much of a chance in her first outing at Pikes Peak. Many, in fact, doubted that she would even finish the mile-and-sixteenth race. Patty surprised all of them, not only finishing but coming in first.

"Thoroughbred horses are like women," Patty told a reporter who asked the secret of her swiftness. "With some of them, if you *demand* something of them you might as well move the Rock of Gibraltar. But if you *ask* something of them, they'll move that rock!"

That summer Patty traveled throughout Colorado, Wyoming and Montana. She won twenty-nine pari-mutuel races and twelve bush events. At times it was particularly rough. She pulled into Durango one night and every hotel room in town was taken, so she broke out a bale of hay, rolled up in a blanket and slept there. "A male jock can bed down in the stables and nobody cares. But it just isn't the same for me as it is for the men," she said.

The bush meets often proved livelier than the races at the pari-mutuel tracks. They are sometimes referred to as "the quickest crap game on four feet," and they are conducted without benefit of pari-mutuel wagering. Further, the meets are not overseen by a racing commission. "There's no test barn, so you can hit them with a needle in the paddock if you want to," Patty stated. "At the time, I was under contract to a man named T. J. Hazlett, and we had one real good horse named Jet Nurse. We called him three different names —Little Man, Sir Brown and I can't remember the third.

They have Calcutta wagering at these meets. They auction off the Calcuttas. Suppose you have eight horses in the race. You have an auctioneer selling the horses in the race. It depends upon what kind of money there is in the group as to what the Calcuttas sell for. Someone buys a horse for ten dollars. A horse that is a sure winner goes for $100. Others will sell for eighty and fifty. All the money goes into one pool, so the person who pays eighty, if his horse wins, gets the whole pool.

"There might be five pools on each race, and each pool contains a different amount of money. We would have people buy tickets for us at a pool for ten dollars on maybe the first two races before people realized that the horse was Jet Nurse listed under another name."

At the end of the summer Patty went back to New Mexico and was just succeeding in getting mounts there when she broke her collarbone and suffered a concussion. When she was released from the hospital she headed further west to Las Vegas, and then on to California.

Patty walked up and down the shed rows at Santa Anita, Hollywood Park and Delmar, trying to get mounts. But the competition was so heavy in southern California that she quickly realized that as a rookie *and* a woman, there wasn't much chance for her there.

"That was a very depressing time in my life," Patty admits. "I kept thinking of all the things I had given up. I had quit smoking, quit drinking and even quit eating because I was gaining weight. I had my children in New Mexico. I didn't date. All this sacrifice just to get a shot to ride."

After a great deal of introspection, Patty made up her mind to move to Waterford Park because her original contract holder was racing there and she knew that he would put her on some live mounts. She also knew that Waterford Park was no magnet for the really hot-shot jockeys who gravitate toward the glamour tracks such as Santa Anita, Aqueduct and Hialeah.

On Patty's last day at Delmar, she happened to sit down at the same table in the track kitchen with Penny Ann Early. After all the publicity the pretty blonde had received, and after her short-lived career as a professional basketball player, Penny Ann finally got her license, only to learn sadly that once her name was no longer a hot item in the newspapers, there were few people who wanted to put her on their horses. In 1970 she had a total of twelve mounts.

"I had been introduced to Penny Ann when I first came to California," Patty recalls. "But she never bothered with me, never spoke to me. She heard I was leaving and she knew where I was going, but she asked me just the same. When I said Waterford Park, she exclaimed, 'Oh, no! Not Waterford Park! That is the bottom of the bucket. That is absolutely the jumpin' off place of the world!' Then she went on to say, 'My greatest ambition is to beat Shoemaker at a photo finish.' So I said, 'Yes, that would be great if you could only ride enough races to do that.' "

Waterford Park has been good to Patty. From September, 1970, when she arrived to December of that year, she rode twenty-one winners. In 1971 she rode in Ohio, Rhode Island, Massachusetts, Pennsylvania, New Jersey and West Virginia.

Patty rode approximately 830 races and won 130—a record that made her the top female jockey in the country in 1971.

Except for being hospitalized for a knee operation as a result of a throw from a horse in which she severed twenty-one ligaments, 1971 was a very good year.

She made enough money in 1971 and 1972 to enable her to bring her children from New Mexico. While she was delighted to have her family together again, she was concerned that they didn't have a father. And when David West, the horsemen's bookkeeper at Waterford Park, asked her to marry him, she accepted. Patty figured he was the "Old Reliable" type.

Patty Barton has become so used to fighting her own battles and making her own decisions that she is often impatient with people who aren't equally strong, and she soon discovered that in any contest of the wills with West she was the dominant personality.

Despite two unsuccessful marriages, Patty says that she is content with her life as it is now. She has three attractive children whom she adores, and she is working in a profession that she genuinely enjoys.

She recently bought a motel and she is also going to college now, taking tutorial courses at West Virginia Northern Community College in Wierton, by appointment. And in addition to all her interests and activities, she is considering opening a mod boutique in East Liverpool. "I could go up to New York," she says, "and buy clothes two years old, and they would think it was the latest fashion down here."

When she becomes too old to race any more, Patty would

like to settle in Arkansas and buy a farm. "I love that state." She smiles. "It's in the very heart of America.

"Becoming a jockey has surpassed my expectations," she admits happily. "When I signed my contract, I was willing to settle for the very least—just getting to ride. But I am constantly amazed at the fringe benefits I receive. For one thing, I have always enjoyed flying. I get on airplanes now like I used to get on the bus, quite often at the expense of some racetrack or some owner of a horse. I wouldn't ever have seen Montana except for a man wanting me to ride his horse at Futuri."

It is obvious that Patty Barton feels comfortable, that she is indeed really proud to be a jockey. "To me this career I've chosen gives me a great feeling of accomplishment," she says. "Not just when I ride a winner, but also when I'm on a 20-to-1 shot and finish fourth. I don't just sit here and say, 'Well, I've arrived.' This is the one really terrific thing about the racing game. Your goals will never cease. You have your goals of how many you can win in an evening, how many you can win in a week, in a meet, how many you can win in a year, how many you can win in a lifetime. I feel in this way I am a very fortunate person. How many people are able to take a hobby and turn it into a business? There's people making a living doing something they don't particularly care about."

And what if her son Jerry decides that he wants to become a jockey?

Patty paused for a moment and then broke into a wide

grin. "You know, if a boy decides to follow in his father's footsteps and become a football player, that seems okay. But if a boy wants to follow his mother as a jockey, it seems a little funny, doesn't it?"

6

"I get knocked for taking a boy off a horse and putting a girl on. The boys say, 'She's not strong enough.' That's a bunch of bullshit in my book."

—Trainer Beverly Cramer

One thing that all the girl jockeys have in common is having worked some of the less attractive stable jobs before they were permitted to don their silks. Even before the barrier was knocked down by Kathy Kusner, women were quietly infiltrating the backside of American racetracks. They were natural hot walkers, grooms, stable foremen and exercise riders because so few men with any brains or a sense of responsibility would work for such low wages while living under such conditions.

Trainers gnash their teeth in despair when exercise boys fail to show up for an early morning workout. They swear at sloppy grooms and handlers who show little or no patience with expensive, high-spirited animals. And they worry about the drinkers and smokers who may cause a disaster.

There was a time—not long ago—when resentment was high with regard to employing women at racetracks. (Even today, most tracks have a rule: No women on the backside after sundown.) However, as the shortage of reliable stable help became acute, trainers began to place more women on the payrolls. They soon discovered that not only were these girls dependable, but they also seemed to like horses more than the men did.

"We notice a change in the disposition of our horses when they are being groomed by a girl," says Johnny Campo, one of the leading trainers in the nation who makes a point of hiring women for his stable. "Many of the horses we consider skittery and hard to manage become docile when they are handled by a girl. A horse can tell the difference between a girl and a man. A horse differentiates by the smell and the voice." Campo has employed as many as seventeen women at one time, giving rise to the nickname Campo's Harem for his stable.

Employment on shed row is by no means a step forward in all ways toward total equality between men and women. "Some trainers want to have girls in their barn so their male help won't have to travel too far to be serviced," is the opinion of a hard-bitten owner who operates a thirty-horse string at the Meadowlands in Pennsylvania.

Some trainers, of course, adopt the opposite view, that despite the fact that women are better workers, they are still basically a distraction to most of the male help. Preston King, a lanky thirty-two-year-old blond who was the top trainer at Aqueduct in 1972, said that he once hired some women but he wouldn't do it again "because all the boys wanted to take them in the stalls. They were nice girls . . . not exactly innocent. Two of them grabbed a couple of guys."

The Trainer

On a chilly November afternoon, Beverly Cramer, an attractive, black-haired woman of twenty-six, sat as dealer for a game of gin rummy in barn 21 at the Meadows Racetrack. Huddled around the makeshift table, which was actually the top of a wooden box, were three of her friends—Cheryl White, one of Beverly's jockeys, Jim Fuller, a retired trainer who helps around the stable, and Dick Allen, a kind-looking man of fifty-five or so who is a bellboy at Holiday Inn. Mr. Allen, who loves the horses, met Beverly at the racetrack several years ago, and they have become good friends. He asked Beverly if he could spend his vacation sleeping in her tack room, and she obliged.

The walls of the room are blanketed with all kinds of horse equipment—saddles, whips, bridles, blinkers. From the lightbulb dangles a piece of fly paper. The only hint of a feminine presence is a pair of beige pantyhose that hang precariously from a hook where they were casually tossed. In the corner are three hot plates. When Beverly and her friends are low on cash, which is most of the time, she cooks a chicken dinner or makes macaroni and cheese for them.

If it is difficult for a woman to be a jockey, it is at least doubly so for one to become a trainer. "The trainer's the underdog of horseracing," Beverly says. "If a trainer's horse runs bad, he doesn't make any money, but he still has to pay his grooms and hot walkers. You have to pay your feed bills and vet bills and blacksmith bills and for medicine. Just a little pain killer can run you twenty or thirty dollars."

Under racing laws, a trainer assumes all responsibility for his employees and for the horses in his care. Entries, scratches, jock mounts, and claiming and purchasing racehorses are all part of his domain. As a rule, a trainer is a salaried employee who receives, in addition, a share of the purse. A public trainer such as Beverly, however, charges the horse owner a flat fee for training, and she, in turn, is responsible for all the expenses incurred in training that animal.

Beverly became a trainer because of an odd set of circumstances. She grew up in Harpers Ferry, Virginia, where she was injured in an automobile accident when she was sixteen. She received $40,000 as a settlement, and instead of going to college, she invested in a lunch wagon business. After two years of wheeling the cart through office buildings, she decided that she disliked the routine. She was restless. "It was too much of a hassle, and I really wasn't satisfied with it," she said.

Because she had always loved horses, Beverly made up her mind to go into racing as a trainer. She started with one horse. "I bought him for $800 and I made around $600 in seconds and thirds," she said. "But I probably spent a thousand in bills, keeping him and feeding him for a year. Plus the blacksmith and vet bills. He had bad legs and required a lot of work—more than a sound horse."

Today Beverly has twelve horses, most of which are cheap,

rundown fleabags. Since she has so many cheap ones, it's not easy for her to convince owners of quality horses that she is indeed capable of training their stock. And she is constantly pitted against the men trainers in a no-holds-barred competition when it comes to acquiring the good horses.

"If you have a good horse, they'll try to submarine you," Beverly says. "They'll go so far as finding the owner's name and number in the telephone book and then calling him and telling him some big bullshit story about how you're not taking good care of his horse or something. Or else telling him, 'I'll train the horse for two dollars less a day.' "

Of all the problems that beset a trainer, one of the hardest is the jockey. "It's a big problem to get the right jock on the right horse," Beverly admits, "because there is no way that one rider fits every horse you have in the barn. You really have to study a lot of jockeys' forms on a horse before you decide."

Two of the jockeys whom Beverly races most frequently are women, Sandy Schleiffers and Cheryl White. This subjects her to a lot of taunting and criticism from the males, who say that she is perpetuating a female ghetto. "I get knocked for taking a boy off a horse and putting a girl on. The boys say, 'She's not strong enough.' That's a bunch of bullshit in my book."

Another problem that Beverly faces as a woman trainer is not that unusual in the employer-employee relationship: the fact that some men resent the idea of taking orders from her. "I've had several guys work for me," she explains, "and sometimes what happens is that they get a crush on you and they don't want to do their work. I had a kid working for me and he used to follow me around like a little puppy dog. He was like a little baby. He gave the impression to me that I was working for him instead of him working for me. He finally quit because I wouldn't take him to get a haircut."

Beverly Cramer has advice for anyone who wants to become a trainer: "Get good horses. Don't take a bunch of bums. A horse makes a trainer just like a horse makes a jockey. It doesn't cost any more to train and feed a good horse. The bad ones cost more because they require so much more attention."

Then, looking a little wistful, Beverly adds: "I wish before I got started I could have gone with a real good stable. If I worked for somebody good for a year it would have saved me a lot of money."

Mary Elizabeth (Mike) Ryan holds the job that Beverly would love to have. She is right-hand man to Johnny Campo, one of the top trainers at Aqueduct.

"Mike Ryan is the kind of girl a fella would be proud to take home to his mother or to Riva Ridge," wrote Gerald Strine, sportswriter for the *Washington Post* about this fetching charmer of Irish descent who holds the most important position of any woman training thoroughbreds in America.

As Johnny Campo's assistant, Mike often stands in for her boss as trainer. Sometimes Mike will take a second string of horses down South or to Garden State Park.

"He trusts me with a million dollars worth of stock," Mike said in a matter-of-fact voice. When she is training on her own she selects races for the horses and the riders and then checks with Johnny. He gives her a choice of ten jockeys she can select to ride, and then she chooses the horses for them. Right now she has thirty people either directly or indirectly under her at Aqueduct, as some of the responsibility is shared by the stable foreman.

One of her principal responsibilities is getting up in the morning to watch the horses gallop around the practice ring. "I watch the people gallop to make sure the horses aren't sore," Mike says.

Mike performs her job more out of a love for horses than out of any affection for a permanent job as trainer. As Mike sees it, she has all the fun of choosing horses for races and putting them together with jockeys. At the same time she has none of the burden of worrying about making the payroll or hiring and firing help. "If I don't like the way someone is doing something, I'll tell John and he'll take care of it. I hide behind his skirts," she says as her Irish eyes twinkle.

The Vet

"I'm always in the center of the storm," chuckled Caroline Gall, an attractive blonde divorcée, as she tried to make order out of the chaos of her musty cubbyhole office that opens onto the indoor paddock at Waterford Racetrack. Caroline holds the prestigious job of track veterinarian, a post for which she gets a hefty salary of $30,000—plus innumerable headaches.

"It's much more difficult to practice on the track than to have a private practice," Caroline says. "First of all, you are dealing with a moneymaking machine. You aren't just patching up somebody's pet. People with small animals will have blind faith in a veterinarian, but horsemen are different. They know those animals. They travel from track to track and they see many vets. Also, a track vet is doing his job right there with an audience to judge him. In a small animal practice you take your dog in and you leave it there."

As track veterinarian, it is Caroline's job to inspect all incoming horses for disease as well as checking each horse every day to make sure it is racing fit and hasn't been injected with any drugs.

Caroline looks the horses over before and after the race and makes notes on any horse she's noticed that is sore or bleeding. "Some of your best horses won't be absolutely sound," she says. "Any horse that's running hard will develop problems—just like your athletes, Joe Namath, or anybody else. The real sound horses are usually the dogs who never ran fast enough to hurt themselves."

Caroline, who comes from Canada, studied two years of pre-vet and four years at vet school. She then practiced for four years as a racetrack vet prior to her appointment at Waterford Park.

"I'm a racetracker first and then a vet," Caroline says, explaining that her brother is a jockey and that she grew up around a racetrack and worked as a hot walker and trainer.

Caroline's job often inspires envy from other women who are jealous of her cushy salary. She responds with impatience. "If they would just go ahead and do something instead of bitching all the time. I run into housewives who will say, 'I wanted to be a vet but I can't stand chemistry.' Well, I can't stand chemistry either, but I learned it."

The Agent

On a sunny day at Gulfstream Park in New Jersey last fall, a group of jockeys' agents were poring over their copies of *The Racing Form.* Typical of their breed, they wore tattered old raincoats, flashy ties and rundown, unpolished brown shoes. Some had cigars drooping from the sides of their mouths.

Into the huddle breezed a pretty blonde with enough chutzpa and instant charm to make Holly Golightly go dark. Her hair fell to her shoulders over a chocolate brown mink jacket, complete with rhinestone buttons. On her head she wore a velvet beret. On her feet were platform shoes circa 1940. As she talked to the other agents, her long false eyelashes batted up and down, completely mesmerizing the group she had invaded.

Francine Plotnick is a jockey's agent. At twenty-two, she manages veteran jockey Rocky Gabrial and a young bug boy named Allen Owens.

Of all the jobs on the backstretch, one of the rarest to encounter is that of a woman as an agent. According to Francine, she is the only female agent licensed in the state of New Jersey. Perhaps because the agent is expected to huckster a bit as well as to dispense counsel, racetrackers often find it hard to see a woman in this capacity.

This doesn't bother Francine. "I've always been aggressive anyway. I'm a very outgoing, gregarious person."

For an apprentice or a journeyman, nothing is more important than a good agent. And having to rely on a 20 to 25 percent cut of the jockey's earning, agents are often forced to find other sources of income.

"It's like being a theatrical agent," Francine says. "You really have to get out and hustle if you are going to make any money for your client. I make between $150 and $200 a week. A top agent can make $6000 to $7000 a week."

Francine gets to the track between six and six-thirty in the morning, and over cocoa in the track kitchen she starts her daily battle of trying to convince trainers to put Rocky on a horse. She then walks up and down the shed rows. "I hit between twenty to twenty-five trainers every morning," Francine explains.

In the afternoon she carefully watches and studies races. She studies the condition book, trying to figure out which horses would be best for Rocky to ride. She spends time on the racing charts, checking horses that were claimed, knowing horses that won and can take a class jump, and horses that are dropping in class. She also needs to understand people and know individual trainer's styles.

Francine's background pointed toward the track. After graduating from Philadelphia's Walter Biddle Saul High School of Agriculture and Horticulture, she worked as hot walker, pony girl and exercise girl.

Despite the fact that her life revolves around the backstretch, she maintains that she does not make a policy of socializing with racetrackers because she feels, as many girl jockeys do, that it would compromise her professional status. "I wouldn't want anybody to think I was going out with a trainer for profit," she explains. "It would be just as if you saw a boxer out with a hood."

The Groom

"I start working at four in the morning, and a lot of times I don't get finished until seven at night. When you keep hours like that, you don't have much time for social life," says Mary Ann Clark, a slim, brown-haired girl with a refined air who works as a groom under trainer Bryan Webb's shed row. Mary Ann is so exhausted from each day's work that most nights she eats dinner prepared by Mrs. Webb at her boss's apartment because she doesn't have enough energy left to cook for herself.

Mary Ann is considerably overqualified for her seven-day-a-week job, which has a base pay of $125 and no retirement benefits. A graduate of the New York State University at Plattsburg, Mary Ann was well on her way toward earning a master's degree in elementary education and guidance counseling when a friend offered her a job grooming horses in Tampa, Florida.

Now, three years later, even though her relatives keep pleading, "Couldn't you just buy a horse and keep it and do something normal?" Mary Ann is hooked. She knows that it's not a practical long-term career goal. "How old can you be and still do this?" she asks.

The job of the groom is probably the most important as far as getting the horses to the races. The work includes feeding, watering, brushing, cleaning, bathing, mucking stalls and bedding down the horse as well as putting the bridle and saddle on the horse before the race.

While grooming horses sounds menial to most people, it actually requires several skills, such as specialized methods for rubbing down and bandaging horses. As he rubs down the horse, a groom can often detect if something is bothering the animal. If he rubs him the same way every day and it bothers him in a spot where it never bothered him before, he knows there's something wrong. "It took me a good year before I could detect the basic illnesses," Mary Ann said.

The job also carries a great deal of responsibility in that the groom spends more time and attention on these valuable horses than anyone else at the track—including the trainers. "Thoroughbred horses get better care than most people's kids do," Mary Ann says. "If he doesn't eat his breakfast, you instantly stick a thermometer in him."

Exercise Girl

"I learned more on the farm than I learned on the track in three years," says Jenny Harmsen, a stocky thirty-year-old Dutch girl who has led a fascinating life as a result of her interest in horses. She is now galloping them in New Orleans, making about $750 a month.

The farm Jenny is referring to is Hobeau Farms, a beautiful 2500-acre breeding ground of neatly trimmed hedges and well-fenced paddocks for thoroughbreds. It is located in Ocala, Florida, 300 miles north of Miami. Hobeau Farms is owned by millionaire Jack Dryfus and managed by a tough foreman named Elmer Heubeck.

The Dryfus breeding farm is run largely by women, and it provides an excellent opportunity for a girl to train as an exercise rider since she can start out by breaking yearlings. "If you don't know nothing, they teach you good here," was the opinion of one Danish girl who works as foreman of the breeding barn.

It takes two years to become a competent exercise rider and many times a girl won't get a chance to perfect her style on the track because trainers have too little time to coach the girls, while on the farm the pace is more leisurely. A big part of her job is to judge the horse while galloping or working it. She looks for such things as how easy the horse is going, whether he's tough to handle or whether he's having trouble breathing or concentrating. The real problem occurs when a horse stops doing things well that he's done well before— things like breaking, switching leads and speeding up and slowing down when you want him to.

Mr. Heubeck doesn't need to worry about help, for he is deluged with applications from girls who want to work at the farm. Several years ago he placed an ad in *Western Horseman* and received over 600 replies. "I'm still using answers from that ad," he says proudly. "Some of the girls wrote to me when they were only twelve years old."

Mr. Heubeck uses a lot of "green girls" at one time, but now he just doesn't have the time to train them. "They almost all have a horse of their own, and they bring it along and board it somewhere nearby."

If he did have the necessary time, he would prefer training the girls himself because he thinks that most equestrian classes don't teach galloping properly. "Some of my best girls have come from the five-and-ten-cent store," he says of the unschooled greenies whom he has trained, adding that formal education is no barrier when it comes to employment. "I've got girls who are college graduates and ones with masters' degrees."

Girls who work at the farm live in dorms and take their meals in a common cafeteria that serves food at cut-rate prices. The workday starts at six in the morning and lasts until four-thirty in the afternoon, with an hour's break for lunch. During the week the girls get half a day off, as well as every other Sunday. Once a month they are off for an entire weekend. The starting salary is $300 a month, and the maximum wage is $500 a month.

Why does he hire so many girls? Is Mr. Heubeck an active promoter of the rights of women? Well, not exactly. "You can knock girls around better," he says. "Boys are harder to handle."

The Valet

"It all started when Mr. Skinner came up to me one day and asked me if I wanted to be famous," explains Terry Cutshaw, a pretty, twenty-seven-year-old housewife who has the unusual distinction of being the first female valet in the history of horse racing.

Bill Skinner, manager of the jockeys' room at the Meadows racetrack, said that hiring Terry was no gimmick. "It's come to the point there are so many female riders you need somebody to take care of them," he said. When he hired Terry last fall, there were five women jockeys racing at the track.

As a jockey's valet, Terry is responsible for cleaning the riders' silks and boots and for laying out the correct outfit, hat and sleeve number to correspond with post positions. She is also responsible for making weight adjustments for the jockeys. There is only a nineteen-minute span between races, which means that if a girl is riding in several races, it would be very difficult for her to do everything herself.

One night last fall at the Meadows, Pinkie Smith rode a full card of nine races; without Terry's assistance she might never have made it. For one race she might have been assigned 120 pounds, so she would need a leaded pad and a big saddle. The next race she might ride at 112 pounds; to make that weight she would need only a rubber pad and a light saddle.

For her labors Terry earns three dollars a mount. Much of her job, however, is acting as a lady-in-waiting to the riders. To set herself up in the job, she laid out $100 for supplies:

brushes, saddle soap, towels and washcloths. She also keeps on hand a supply of lotions, powders, deodorants, Kleenex, perfumes and razors.

Terry enjoys her work, but she is quick to point out that it has its drawbacks. "Some of these girls just throw their clothes on the floor. I won't put up with that."

The Pony Girl

"Montana's not my real name," Farrel Warren announces as she scrubs mud off the belly of her dirty white pony one morning at Monmouth Park in Oceanport, New Jersey. "Folks just call me Montana 'cause that's where I come from." Then she adds, "Sometimes they call me Scrappie 'cause I get in a fight every now and then. But I'm a lot better than I used to be. I've only been in three fights since I came East."

A souvenir from one of Montana's battles is etched diagonally across her face—a scar on her right cheek that was put there a month before when a stable boy did his crude art work with a fingernail. She had been kind to him, transporting his horse from track to track in one of her trailers and occasionally lending him money. But one day, as Montana phrases it, "He called me a profane name, and I just blew my top and let him have it. He was kickin' and bitin' and scratchin' just like a girl. Where I come from, we call that chickenshit fightin'."

Montana's heritage is part Cree Indian; she grew up on a farm in Cut Bank, Montana. She came to the East from the

West Coast. Her job as a pony girl enables her to travel a lot, and she has taken advantage of that freedom by criss-crossing the country from racetrack to racetrack, going north as far as Canada and south as far as Mexico.

The work of the pony girl might seem monotonous and unchallenging to some, but it is a vital part of racing. Just before a race, a horse is led by a strap that is held by a pony boy or girl during the post parade. Thoroughbreds are "highly strung" animals that often become nervous before a race. If a horse were to run off, he might waste a lot of his strength and energy and then perform poorly. Trainers often use pony girls or boys in the morning on horses that they want to exercise but not tire.

Montana is paid ten dollars for each horse she ponies to the gate before a race, and she averages four or five a day. She is also paid for the horses that she exercises in the morning. In addition to this income, Montana owns five horses, one of which races and brings in approximataely 6 or 7 thousand dollars a year.

She has managed her money well, socking enough away in her action-packed twenty-seven years to buy a two-horse and a four-horse trailer and to start dabbling in real estate. "I'm gettin' me a piece of land," she says, adding that she is in the process of buying five acres in Fort Lauderdale. "Two things they can't take away from you, education and a piece of land," she offers in her country wisdom. Besides owning land, she will someday also possess a bachelor's degree, for she is only twenty-four credits away from receiving one from Montana State University, where she majored in commercial art.

Don Levine, one of the trainers for whom Montana freelances, can't get over his pony girl's prosperity. "Montana's doing better than I am," he says kiddingly. "The other day I said to her, 'Montana, will you marry me?'"

But Montana's not the marrying kind, at least not any more, and at least not now. "What the hell do I need a man for?" she asks as she brushes a braid behind her face. "You can get *that* for free with no strings attached."

She was married once—for a month and a half—to a fellow with the curious name of Crystal. "I figured it was the first one, and I ought to try to make it last," she explains.

Crystal was no shining light. He was a loafer. She and her husband were working on a farm in Wrey, Colorado, Montana says, and things were pretty good for six weeks. "I had twenty-five head of horses in the paddock and two hundred in the pasture. And my old man runs off to town and gets drunk. I figured, by God, if he can get drunk, so can I! So I walked into the bar where he was sittin' on a stool drinkin' vodka, and I asked him for twenty dollars. He said, 'Get it from the boss.' Well, I figured that any man who can't give his old lady twenty dollars isn't worth having. So I took the vodka and poured it all over his head. Then I grabbed Crystal by his shirt collar and dragged him out to the street and started jumpin' up and down on top of him. It took three guys to pull me off him."

Montana stops talking for a moment, just long enough to let a whisper of a blush come to her face. It was an awkward reaction in the context of the conversation, and yet so ironically feminine.

Then she picks up a water bucket and starts to walk away, slowly. Over her shoulder she says, "I don't like to tell too many stories about myself because it reflects on my character."

7

*"I think it's unavoidable that many of these girls have a
pretty strong dose of what's been called penis envy"*

—Dr. Natalie Shainess, a Manhattan psychiatrist and an
outspoken feminist, commenting on female jockeys.

What *is* this thing with women and horses?

Parents, teachers, owners of horses, trainers—all comment
routinely, it seems, about the almost mystical bond or fixation that exists between women and equines. Many treat it
as a typical phenomenon of nature, like the rising and falling
of the tides. Yet few ask why.

In talking with women who work at racetracks, one has
the feeling that while they don't dislike men, they regard
them as peripheral. Their attention centers on horses. Given
the choice between Gregory Peck and Man o' War, they'd
take Man o' War.

In a previous chapter, I discussed the sexual exploitation
of women by trainers, and it is only appropriate that one
should look at the situation from the other side of the mirror
and then pointedly ask, Who is the exploiter and who is the
exploited? Most trainers, it is assumed, have some sort of

affection for horses, or they wouldn't be involved in the world of racing. The profession is far too risky, too unsteady, and too exhausting for one to enter merely for the money. The long hours and the seven-day-a-week schedule, coupled with all the travel needed for moving from track to track with the seasons, cause these men to become ghetto inhabitants of their profession.

Trainers usually have few close friends off the track, and the gypsy mobility of their work often causes them to grow apart from their wives. They are, therefore, psychologically predisposed to become attracted to women on the back-stretch, if only because these women share their interest in horses. And a woman who wants mounts may be willing to "stoop to conquer." She is more reluctant when it comes to giving her heart.

At one track I made the acquaintance of a petite, brown-haired jockey in her early twenties. She works for a nervous, middle-aged trainer who chainsmokes Pall Malls and is constantly on the telephone because the horses he looks after are managed by a group of six persons, and he has to keep each one informed as to the horses' health and their fitness to race. He is married to a plump, complacent woman whose life centers on their four children. And he doesn't see her or them often.

So his pretty jockey is his fond fondant, his literal pride and joy. During morning workouts, he leans over the rail at the track and watches her gallop his horses, and he stares at her just like a young boy with a crush.

She is fully aware of the power involved in being a horse

trainer's darling. "For a man, any man, who loves horses," she says, "there's something very sensual about seeing a woman he cares about riding an animal that he trains. I can't really explain it. It's just something you sense . . . he feels, like, the three of us are sharing something that is very physical."

But as she talks about the trainer, it becomes apparent that she considers him as something that she can control, just like the horses she races. There is not the slightest trace of romance or tenderness when she talks about their relationship. "He lets me ride his horses, so I let him stick it in," is the succinct way she explains their relationship.

At another track in a different state, I met a trainer who says that he has been intimate with several jockeys. He is lean and handsome and rakish, and it's apparent that this man doesn't need a string of horses as a come-on for seducing a woman; yet he has to admit that the women jockeys he has known "have him stumped." Over a martini, he confided, "They're one-man women for the length of the meet, but if another trainer offers to put them on better horses for the next meet, they'll go with him." And there is in the well of his eyes the loneliness of a man who has spent many nights lying in bed next to a woman whose thoughts were miles away.

The horse fixation is, of course, not limited to women who become jockeys or to those who work at the tracks as grooms and hot walkers. The estimated ratio of girls to boys among those who take riding instruction is nearly seven to one. Nor is this so-called horse preoccupation limited to the young. Psychiatrists often see the same monomania for horses exhibited by conservative-looking, middle-age women who participate in hunts, all decked out to the nines in their pinks.

In a survey conducted by the New York State Department of Education during the late 1960's, grammar school children were asked to name the animal they would like to be. Lions or tigers were usually selected by the boys; the overwhelming choice of the girls was the horse.

Dr. Herbert Wieder, a practicing psychoanalyst in the state of New York, who has done extensive work with both young girls and mature women who manifest a preoccupation with horses, commented about the survey: "Little boys often equate sadism with masculinity. Little girls often have the opposite view: that sadism means to be hurt, to be attacked by a sadistic male. The girl would be attracted to the strong but gentle, non-attaching horse, and the boy would feel himself to *be* the attacking, fearless lion—Richard the Lionhearted."

Dr. Wieder elaborated on the child-animal relationship. "The child regards the animal as his equal and feels akin to him. Actually, animals can do lots of things that little children aren't allowed to do. They can soil; they can wet. And they can attack. They have a kind of unbridled physical life which the little child has to bring under control, so that the children admire animals for having that freedom.

"To children, animals can represent family members. They can represent themselves as a baby. And they can represent parts of their own body. After a while, animals can represent sexual or aggressive drives, such as the lion symbolizing power and hostility. The elephant usually represents something kind and gentle and loving. The bear, a paternal figure.

"Take Milne's *Winnie the Pooh*, for example. It's a very beautiful literary piece that represents the psychology of children. *Winnie the Pooh* contains animals that act like people. They talk, they respond, they get into trouble. It's a family in which you can discern a father, a mother and children. The big animals can be either mother or father."

Mary Bacon recalls that as a child she considered horses her closest confidants: "I used to have this one horse named 'Timber Top.' People would ask me who my best friend was, and I'd say, 'Oh, Timber Top.'"

Many of the women jockeys have said that while horses are their favorite animals, they feel a strong affinity to other pets as well.

Donna Hillman has owned pet mice, rats, foxes, a rabbit, a twelve-foot cobra and a bobcat. "The bobcat snipped the rear out of my landlady's dress," she laughs. "I didn't stay at that place long!" She's also owned an olingo, which is related to a panda. And now she owns a Great Dane, a German Shepard and a horse.

According to Dr. Wieder, animals are often used to discharge aggression on the one hand and sexual tension on the other. A child will endow animals with various feelings that he has, so that the animals thus become a way of dealing with feelings that cannot be handled or discharged adequately in any other way. A child might strike a dog as a means of expressing hostility toward a sibling or a parent, because the dog, to him, can represent anyone. "Children past the age of three often regard animals as genitals," related Dr. Wieder. "They play with the animal's private parts," he said. "They will poke around. They'll pinch."

Boys who are interested in horses show a marked drop when they hit puberty, according to Dr. Wieder, while girls retain their interest. Many girls will keep that interest until some boy comes into their life. Then the horse relationship diminishes. "But for a particular number of girls," Dr. Wieder added, "the horse overrides a relationship with a boy, and the interest in the animal takes precedence to relationships with human beings. For some it becomes a very urgent and persistent activity."

Many psychiatrists contend that horseback riding is a popular way of masturbating for girls. Dr. Gerald H. Pearson published a paper a few years ago in the *Psychoanalytic Quarterly* in which he said: "A girl, because of the nature of her genitals, is more accustomed than the boy to obtaining genital sensations from such activities as sliding down a banister, rubbing against the corner of a table, and thus would get greater genital sensations from riding."

One woman jockey in Maryland does not dispute this theory. "Riding enabled me to lose my virginity in the nicest possible way," she confessed.

Psychiatrists say that a girl who has an affinity for horses invariably has a strong attachment to her father. The horse has the qualities a girl seeks in her father: strength, power and gentleness. And because one of the earliest recollections a young girl has is of riding on her father's shoulders, she thus associates horseback riding with her father.

Many girls think of the horse as their genital, other doctors contend. It is big and extended and she becomes part of the animal.

Dr. Natalie Shainess, a New York City psychiatrist and an active feminist, expressed her views as follows: "I think it's unavoidable that many of these girls have a pretty strong dose of what's been called penis envy. The kind of superior strength and skill that being a jockey calls for and the roughhouse of competition suggests a strong feeling that the male world, the active world, is the thing that holds worth and not much else of anything does."

"Who says it's a man's world?" is Sandy Schleiffer's answer to such opinions.

When I commented to Dr. Shainess that penis envy seemed like an old-fashioned concept in light of the women's liberation movement, she said, "My belief is that true penis envy— I mean a really angry competition, jealousy and, one might say, hatred of men but at the same time a desire to be like them and do everything they do—has very early roots. Unless it has early roots within the family, it isn't penis envy."

As an example, Dr. Shainess related Patty Barton's anecdote about her grandmother's asking her what she wanted to be when she grew up. When Patty replied, "Gene Autry," her grandmother washed the little girl's mouth out with soap.

"This child did what every little girl does," Dr. Shainess said. "She was watching a show and she didn't feel bound to identify with the woman, which is only natural. Anyone of any sex would like to be the hero, particularly when the hero is portrayed as a much more glamorous figure than the heroine. So her longing to be Gene Autry, you see, was perfectly natural. What her grandmother did was extremely painful; the reaction indicated 'Goddamn it. You're a girl!' Here is an intensely traumatic situation to a child. Having your mouth washed out with soap is painful and it's done forcefully, and to have this happen as a result of something that she cannot conceive as wrong is hurtful."

Logically, then, if the driving force behind a female jockey is penis envy, what's behind male jockeys? Dr. Wieder suggested: "The male jockey is an interesting guy, too. He often feels himself to be more like an appendage that attaches itself to some big woman. I mean, one of the things that some jockeys have a propensity for is the big woman. I guess he has to, since there aren't many his size. This has always been a kind of humorous cartoon, and it reflects as well the feeling of the jockey as not being a man completely intact. The need to be attached to a woman gives him a body. He is like one big penis, and that penis is disengaged; his horse replaces the body.

"It can also be the woman that he is now astride and riding. The concepts big, strong, powerful represent father to both boy and girl. But there is also the corresponding attitude that the horse is something big that can carry. Something that will be embraced, something that is protective, which can also be maternal. A boy will often take the big animal and act and experience feelings that belong to the mother."

While a boy may have these feelings, it rarely develops into the monomania that occurs when girls become emotionally involved with horses.

"If you think of the phrase 'wild horses' that used to be popular some years ago," Dr. Shainess explained, "it has the symbolic impression of unbridled feeling and unbridled passion. So I would say that it is often girls, who are in fear of their developing sexuality and have a great conflict over it during adolescence, who turn to a kind of 'acting out' in which horses become almost a monomania. It's the only thought in their heads. It's like gamblers. They will never get over it. As their interest turns to horses and grows, it increasingly becomes part of their general life style.

"And it's also an escape from other things, so it's as though they have one overdeveloped maneuver, one overdeveloped way of living that eliminates other things. Instead of trying to deal with these areas, what they have done is to avoid them, as if they let one arm become paralyzed through disuse and overdeveloped the other. For women with a horse fixation, all their life revolves around it. All information that is taken in . . . it's as if it goes through a special funnel. They take in the horse information and they spit out anything else."

Mary Bacon admits that she hides behind horses. They are her protection against the world. "Horses are just like people —only better," she says.

Dr. Shainess found it appropriate that many of the top women jockeys came from broken homes. Mary Bacon's father had a breakdown, and she was placed in a foster home; Robyn Smith was in and out of foster homes; Patty Barton is an orphan; Sandy Schleiffers, Pinkie Smith, Jennifer Rowland, Barbara Jo Rubin and Donna Hillman all have divorced parents.

Children from broken homes, Dr. Shainess remarked, are often attracted to roving kinds of organizations such as the rodeo, the circus and the racetrack because they give the person a sort of family in a large sense. This is particularly true for those who have been in foster homes. The rodeo or the circus or the track have a superficial camaraderie that acts as a magnet to the homeless, rootless, unbound individual who is somewhat afraid of depth involvements because he has never really known or experienced them.

"I think also that for women who hang around a racetrack, particularly those who want to be jockeys, there is a longing for men while, at the same time, there is a need to compete with them. They need to try to enter a man's world, to try to *be* like a man. Simultaneously, they are denying their longing to have an emotional relatedness to a man, and they can play both sides of the record that way and never get too involved."

The equine-obsessed woman is sometimes touched upon in literature, and much of this material views the phenomenon from a different viewpoint than the psychiatric profession. Are women who are labeled "horse freaks" experiencing the throes of penis envy, or are they simply reacting to the fact that modern men are not masculine enough?

D. H. Lawrence deals with this theme in his novella *St. Mawr.* He describes a strong, self-assertive woman, Lou Witt, who sees in her horse, St. Mawr, many of the good qualities that her husband lacks. To her the animal is "fierce," "potent" and "undominated." The man who holds a position in the world but who has little *force de frappe* on the sexual front is a favorite Lawrence theme, and it might have application to women who have a horse fixation. So many men in business today have come to settle for false gods that their only potency is in manipulating the things of the world, those things that have become "too much with us." They pay little genuine attention, if any, to the true potency involved in a man-woman relationship, and often they are interested not in sexual passion but in sexual compulsion. Achievement is nothing unless it can be measured.

Lou Witt's basic dislike of men sprung from this disappointment. "I don't hate men because they're men, as nuns do. I dislike them because they're not men enough: babies and playboys, and poor things showing off all the time, even to themselves. I don't say I'm any better. I only wish, with all my soul, that some men were bigger and stronger and deeper than I am."

The sexual attraction of women for horses is integral in Robinson Jeffers' poem "The Roan Stallion," where a young married woman of Spanish and Indian descent makes sexual overtures to a horse. At one point she crushes her breast to the animal and moans, "If I could bear you. No way, no help, a gulf in nature." (There is a dearth of literature and psychological writing about horses making passes at women.)

In an exegesis on the poem by Jeffers, Dr. Shainess gave an interpretation of the horse fixation: "The symbolic use of the horse seems to me that here was a woman who was leading a lonely and degraded life with a man who was neither human nor decent. The beautiful horse began to symbolize for her, you might say, the male principle of beauty:

that is, the beauty of the spirit in its wildness. (It is this same beauty that audiences have found so appealing in such recent movies as *Butch Cassidy and the Sundance Kid* and the Clint Eastwood films.) You could say it was a kind of fusion in her because it represented a freedom that she longed to share. It took a sexual direction, one might say, because she experienced sex only in what can be termed rape. In other words, it was not a sex of mutuality; what she wanted was sex that could be the result of her desire and her choice, giving her some volition in the sexual act. Since there wasn't a decent man to have fantasies about, the horse, rightly or wrongly, became her choice—a beautiful, wild, free creature that she could choose to participate with. Call it an insane fantasy if you wish, but contained therein is the essence of her problem: her loss of humanness as a woman, no respect for her as anything except an object to be used in every way, sexually and as a servant and cook. But not ever appreciated."

In the course of writing this book, I have often wondered whether female jockeys are simply a slim phenomenon, a side path toward women's liberation. Or are they actually the test pilots for a new evolutionary stage?

It cannot be denied that a racetrack provides a fascinating microcosm for the war between the sexes. It is a tight world of relatively uneducated people, most of whom belong to a class that still clings strongly to cultural stereotypes regarding the roles of men and women. Thus the question is not whether women are physically capable of competing against men, since in most instances men simply by virtue of their superior strength will command the edge. Rather, what happens when men and women compete directly against each other and when women compete against women, not merely for the favor and attention of a member of the opposite sex but for self-glory, status and economic gain after the veneer of society has been stripped to the grain.

In *Slouching Toward Bethlehem*, Joan Didion writes about a persistent childhood dream of wanting to grow up and meet a man like John Wayne, a rugged, take-charge sort who would always protect her. Didion describes how Wayne, in a movie called *War of the Wildcats*, promised the heroine that he would build her a house "at the bend of the river where the cottonwoods grow." The world of John Wayne is a world where he is in command, where he gives the orders: "Let's ride! Saddle up!" "I'm in charge around here! You men fire when I tell you to!" An important part of the John Wayne myth is that there will always be a good, virtuous woman loyally waiting for him when he returns from his confrontations with the bad guys; and as soon as he gets back, he'll build that home.

Young, impressionable girls who watch old Westerns can choose to be either the pretty, slightly buxom woman in calico who stands on the front porch of her daddy's farmhouse waiting for her conquering hero, or she can be the sanitized, Goody Two-Shoes who wears lots of fringe and sings off-key, like Dale Evans. But if you have a streak of imagination and adventure, coupled with a taste for the wild, it is obvious that the John Waynes and the Hopalong Cassidys had a lot more fun and excitement out there with cattle thieves and posses than the women did in their flour-sack dresses at kitchen sinks.

It is not just the John Waynes who have all the fun and excitement in American folklore; it is the Ernest Hemingways and the Errol Flynns and the Joe Namaths. It is always the men who are brawling writers, soldiers of fortune, lecherous athletes and spies. The blood-and-guts world of men is the exciting one.

Now the tomboys are coming out of the woodwork, proving that for some women, at least, the passive role is alien. People like Mary Bacon and Patty Barton are establishing a pattern for a new folk image where women are actively adventurous.

Patty Barton didn't dream of growing up and marrying Gene Autry—she wanted to *be* Gene Autry. And after two marriages, one to a real-life cowboy, she has now saved her money and bought a motel, which in a sense is her house "at the bend of the river." In the meantime, Joan Didion admits that there has never been a John Wayne in her life. So even though it may not be quite the popular fantasy, Patty Barton's daydream has come closest to being realized. For while Joan Didion dreamed of being rescued, Patty Barton dreamed of taking care of herself.

This is true also for Mary Bacon, who with her devil-may-care attitudes is far more liberated than, say, the garden-type feminist, because she has the tough guts to be in charge of her own life. She is not a parasite, leeching off someone else's achievements and then turning around to complain about her loss of "freedom," as so many women do.

Perhaps her assertiveness goes back to the disappointment in modern men described by Lawrence and Jeffers in *St. Mawr* and "The Roan Stallion." When Mary was at Fairgrounds in New Orleans, she was training horses as well as riding them. An old racetracker noticed her Toronado and, with a crude ignorance that is not exactly unknown among his type, asked, "You got some man supporting you to be able to afford a car like that?"

"Yeah," Mary retorted. "He's got four legs and he's standing in barn 43. Name's John the Hiker. All you got to do is hit him on the ass and he runs. You hit a two-legger in the ass and he just stands there."

GLOSSARY OF RACING TERMS

Across the board: Horse is played to win (1st), place (2nd), show (3rd). Win collects all three positions; second collects place and show; third collects third money.

Allowance race: A nonclaiming race where the weight assigned to a horse depends upon the time that has elapsed since its last win and on the amount of money received for previous winnings.

Apprentice allowance: A weight allowance given, except in handicap races, to a jockey who has been riding less than one year.

Backstretch: Straightaway on the far side of a racetrack.

Bear out: Go wide on the turns.

Beat the bushes: To race in cheaper circuits.

Blinkers: Eye shades placed at the sides of a horse's eyes so that he can see only straight ahead.

Boat race: A race wherein participants collaborate illegally to determine winner beforehand.

Break his maiden: To win his first race; this term is used to refer either to a jockey or a horse.

Breeze a horse: When a rider works a horse the same way a jockey does in a race. That is, he crouches down on the animal and lets him run at full speed.

Bug boy: Apprentice jockey eligible for weight allowance.

Bush meet: Small racetracks often without inside railings and frequently situated on fairgrounds, which are not subject to the jurisdictions of state racing commissions. There is no pari-mutuel wagering.

Buzzer: An electrical device which shocks a horse into going faster. Also called a "machine" or a "joint."

Calcutta: A form of gambling in which participants bid for the horses entered in a race; the proceeds from which are put into a pool for distribution according to a pre-arranged scale of percentages.

Caliente helmet: A helmet made of high impact resistant material with a rubber-lined interior and a chin strap.

Chestnut: A reddish-colored horse with same color tail, mane and points.

Claiming race: A race in which all horses entered may be claimed (purchased) before the race at a previously established (claiming) price.

Clocker: Person using a stopwatch to time a horse's workout.

Colors: The owner's silks worn by the jockey.

Colt: A male horse under the age of five.

Combination ticket: A ticket in which the bettor picks the horses he thinks will run first, second or third (win, place or show in track parlance); a combination ticket generally is known as betting "across the board."

Condition book: The track secretary's schedule of races for a race meeting and specifications for each race coming up.

Cooler: Light blanket to cover a racehorse; it helps prevent colds and tightening of muscles after exercise.

Daily double: System of picking the winner of the first two races; the bettor wins only if both selections win.

Dead heat: Two or more horses finishing a race in a tie.

Drugstore handicap: Drugs used in a race.

Educated currency: Money placed on a horse as a result of supposed authentic information.

Entry: Two or more horses in the same race under one owner or trainer.

Exacta: System of pool betting on two horses in the same race. To win, horses must finish first and second exactly as played.

Fast track: When track is firm and horses run in fast time.

Favorite: The horse or entry quoted at the lowest odds at post time.

Filly: Female horse under the age of five.

Finish line: A high wire across the track representing the finish of a race.

Foal: Newborn horse of either sex.

Furlong: 220 yards, or one-eighth of a mile.

Furlong pole: Pole located one-eighth of a mile from the finish line.

Garrison finish: This means that a horse finished very fast after trailing most of the way. The name comes from Snapper Garrison, a famous former jockey who rode in that manner.

Gelding: Unsexed (castrated) male horse.

Handicap: In a handicap, the weight assigned to a horse depends on its record. The better a horse is, the more weight it must carry.

Handle: Total money wagered on a race or on an entire card.

Home stretch: Straightaway to the finish line in front of the stands.

Hot walker: One who walks horses to cool them off after gallop, work or race.

In the money: A horse that finishes first, second or third.

Inquiry: When the stewards examine a race film or question jockeys in a race to determine if an infraction of the rules occurred.

Irons: Stirrups.

Jockey Weight: From 110 to 115 pounds. A horse can carry no less than 86 and/or as high as the handicapper wishes.

Jockeys Up: Announcement by track official for jockey to mount horse, usually in walking ring.

Juvenile: A two-year-old horse.

Live mount: A horse which has a good chance of winning.

Lugging in or runs out: Horse pulling toward the left or right while running on the track.

Maiden: Any kind of horse that never has won a race.

Mare: A female horse aged five or older.

Morning glory: A horse that works out brilliantly in the morning but performs poorly in a race in the afternoon.

Oat muncher: A horse that does not pay for its feed with its winnings.

Objection: When owner, trainer or jockey complains to stewards for examination of film or jockeys to determine if a foul was made during the race.

On the nose: This expression means betting to win only.

Overland route: A horse that races wide around the track.

Overnight: List of horses and jockeys for upcoming race. The overnight sheet comes out either 24 or 48 hours before a race.

Paddock: The enclosure where horses are saddled thirty minutes before post time.

Paddock judge: The person responsible for getting the jockeys on their mounts on time.

Pari-mutuel: System of wagering controlled by automatic electronic computers.

Parlay: A single wager on two or more horses for first, second or third position. Total payoff is wagered on other horses named after first wager wins; the entire wager is lost if one horse loses.

Patrol film: Motion picture of entire race. These films are viewed by stewards for infractions of racing rules. A pan shot and front view.

Patrol judge: Official of track, usually elevated at vantage point in order to observe horses and riders during a race for infractions of race rules.

Perfecta: Separate wagering pool on two horses in the same race to run first and second; this must be a perfect selection to win.

Photo finish: A photograph is examined to ascertain the positions of the horses at the finish line.

Place: A horse that finishes second.

Plater: A horse that generally competes in cheap races.

Pony boy/girl: Rider on a pony who leads the horse and jockey to the starting gate by means of a strap.

Post parade: Jockeys and horses parading in front of the stands before a race.

Post position: A horse's position in the starting gate from inner rail outward; it is decided by drawing at close of entries the day prior to the race.

Pulled Up: To be forced to stop during a race because of an injury or an accident.

Purse: Total amount of money that designated race is worth.

Push (hand ride): When a jockey pushes on the horse with his hands. The jockey moves with the horse.

Quarter pole: Pole one-quarter mile from the finish line.

Quinella: Separate wagering pool on two horses in the same race to run first and second. If either horse selected wins and the other runs second, the bettor wins.

Ringer: A horse that runs under an assumed name; a good horse is substituted for a lesser one, thereby getting high odds on a good horse. Tattooing has made this practice rare.

Running for a tag: A horse that is entered in a claiming race.

Schooling: Teaching a horse how to enter, start and break from the starting gate in a race.

Scratch: Declare or withdraw a horse from a race in which he has been entered.

Show: A horse that finishes third.

Silks: Racing togs and colors worn by jockeys.

Sire: The male parent of a horse.

Sleeper: A horse that does not race in its best form, in order to deceive the handicappers and the betting public. When the proper time comes, the owner will instruct the jockey to win.

Sloppy track: A track so badly soaked from rain that the surface is covered with mud.

Smart money: Money bet on the right horse.

Spook: A horse that frightens easily.

Sprint race: Any distance up to and including seven furlongs. All races over seven furlongs are distance races.

Sprinter: A horse that shows a sudden burst of speed at the starting gate but then suddenly slows down.

Stakes race: High-class race where each horse's owner puts up money in addition to the purse put up by the track.

Steward: Top official at racetrack with power to fine, suspend and rule off persons licensed in racing.

Tack: Racing equipment.

Totalisator board: Equipment on infield that indicates the progress of the betting, supplies probable winning odds and reveals the payoff after the race is official.

Tote board: Electronic computer that totals bets in separate pools for win, place and show; it determines and prints odds and payoff prices. Time of race, post time, time of day and order of finish are other features.

Tout: A person may tout a horse by giving tips.

Track conditions: Fast—dry, even footing.
> Muddy—soft, wet.
> Heavy—drying track.
> Sloppy—after rain.
> Slow—damp, clinging.

Weanling: A baby horse removed from mare and mare's milk.

Wire: The finish line.

Workouts: Time trials, usually held shortly after daybreak and occasionally between races in the afternoon.

Yearling: A horse under the age of two.

DAT